Way More Than A Bed On Stilts is written for the person or fan in a crowded living space. It shows them more options to cope with their pressing needs, through creative and practical furnishings. If a strategy of life improvement includes basic needs, plus education, organization and discipline, we must accommodate those continually. Of course we need a bed, but we also need to store our clothes in a ready to wear condition. Yes, we need education, but we also need a place to study and an organized way to store and access our study materials.

If we lack a clothes closet, or bureau, or a desk, organized storage, or the space for it, we handicap ourselves! *Way More Than A Bed On Stilts* can help people overcome these types of limitations.

This book contains a 21st century loft bed design. When built and used as designed, it is safe; it exceeds all applicable safety standards. Please read those standards and evaluate for yourself. This loft bed design is very durable. It won't become shaky in a year or two. The frame should serve for many years. It can be disassembled and reassembled repeatedly to accommodate moving.

This loft bed system is incredibly useful: it features multiple options for built in desks, shelving, drawers and containers. It accommodates clothes storage, books, files, supplies, games and lighting. The design is modular; the accessory options fit together in several combinations. On top of all this, more than one may fit in a room! This system is designed for most of the electronic accoutrements of modern life. This is the 21st century.

Way More Than A Bed On Stilts is a do-it-yourself project. If you are at all handy, you can build this, while saving money. The sample configuration loft bed with a desk, bureau, and closet rod cost about the same as a comparable size bureau alone (excluding the mattress of course). This is do-able for many people. Just follow the instructions and choose wisely. You can do it!

Way More than a Bed on Stilts!

Erik Johanson

Way More than a Bed on Stilts

This book is dedicated to my friends at CVII. They are not just talking about making the world a better place, they are doing it!

I want to thank my parents, Don and Lynn. I especially wish to recognize the long support of my soul mate Peg. I also thank the many friends who encouraged me to write this and complete it.

The "way more" concept is essentially getting more for your money and efforts. In its highest form, it goes well beyond bargain hunting and prioritization. It requires thinking things through and evaluating the contribution of every aspect toward larger goals. Frugality is recognized as a virtue. Doing it yourself is a time honored tactic. I assert that a better result can often be achieved while consuming fewer resources. I know this is a radical departure from mainstream consumerism and advertising today (think shiny, brittle plastic)! Some have called this "poor man's wisdom". I call it timely.

So, what is a loft bed, and who would want one? A loft bed is a specialized form of bed, which has an elevated sleeping platform. This makes room for another function beneath it. A loft bed effectively increases the available space. Young adults and college students have historically used these the most. The concept is also adaptive to families with teenagers, and economically challenged households. A well built loft bed system will serve more people in smaller rooms and buildings, for increased utility. That means getting more for your housing dollar.

The history of loft beds, in dormitories, goes back several decades. Traditionally, dorm rooms were small, shared, and had very little storage. (Many rented houses and apartments share this problem.) Most of the earliest loft beds were student built and of an experimental nature. Casual research illustrates the development and refinement of the concept from crude, partial, and inadequate, to some minimum standards of structure and use.

The Consumer Products Safety Commission, and the American Society of Testing and Materials, have developed some manufacturer's standards, which apply to loft beds. These regulate the form and spacing of railings, posts, ladders, etc., to ensure safety, by avoiding the worst falling, entrapment and choking hazards. I believe this loft bed design meets or exceeds all those requirements. The CPSC and ASTM websites and references are included in the rear appendix. Please do yourself a favor, and read those standards for yourself. In addition; many colleges have developed their own standards for loft beds used within their property. This design should meet or exceed those as well. Other countries may have developed their own standards. If by some chance this is a stricter safety standard; I definitely recommend you revise to the stricter standard.

I observed many loft beds over the years and concluded that most were wobbly beds on stilts. As a builder, I knew the requirements to prevent a structure from becoming wobbly and unsafe. My biggest bone to pick with most online plans is also true of most manufactured loft beds. Their structure is minimal, and they become shaky and unsafe within a year or so. There is no sway bracing to be found. They are planned to ship in small packages but not to be sturdy. This is unacceptable! Basic geometry points out why this happens. The intertwined concepts of the lever and the triangular brace are sufficient to explain this. The vertical and horizontal structural elements require the diagonal brace to maintain their form and rigidity over time and repeated stressing. Without the brace, leverage works the joint loose. It only gets worse, and more shaky, with more time. (Just think of all those leaning barns and garages you have seen with inadequate bracing.)

This loft bed design does have sufficient bracing to maintain its form. This design has more in common with an open front cabinet than it does with those platforms on stilts. Each of the sides is braced to ensure stability. Like a cabinet, the sides need not be massively heavy. The inherent bracing prevents deflection. Although the loft bed can be assembled and disassembled repeatedly, it becomes sturdy with all of its braces and fasteners secured.

The basic loft bed structure (chapters 1–5) consists of two end frame sub-assemblies, two mattress rail sub-assemblies, and a spreader rail with diagonal braces. A headboard and safety rails complete the package. These sub-assemblies are very strong! The two end frames are permanently assembled, in such a way, that they will remain square for a lifetime. When the loft bed is assembled onsite, the entire back, and half of the front, are solidly braced, plumb, and square. The braces are large enough, and the glue surface area is large enough, to ensure durable stability. The form follows the function!

My safety rails are not cobbled on after the fact either; they are incorporated from the beginning. They exceed the safety standards. They are strong! They are taller than the minimum requirement, and they protect the user on all four sides. No one should fall from normal use!

The lumber of choice is construction grade soft woods, like spruce, pine, and fir. These must be selected for the best appearance, naturally. Since these lumber species and grades are ok for building houses, barns, and stores, they are also strong enough for a small structure like this loft bed! Valuable hardwoods are not used in this design. Should the builder cut a board too short, or otherwise spoil it, so that it is completely unusable; they are only out $5 – $10, for their mistake, not $75. – $100!

The accessories that work with the loft bed are another aspect to consider. As you study the field of competing loft bed designs, you can conclude what the usual features and accessories are. It might have a small desk, with a small book shelf, for an option, or an open space for your futon or beanbag. I think my design goes a lot farther. It is actually a loft bed system, with many accessory options. This do-it-yourself book has multiple desk, shelf, and storage options for clothes, books, files, *CDs*, etc. For many people the storage accessories alone will justify purchasing this book. Where else do you find all this information (and incorporated design) in one place? The bed side table option is way cool and useful. I haven't seen that anywhere else.

What I offer here is not just more and better though, I explain how to build it! The details are simplified, and the process is broken down for the handy person and beginning woodworker. Most people of average aptitude and coordination can build my loft bed system. The detailed explanations with drawings and photographs walk you through all phases of construction. You don't have to settle for a lesser bed, that doesn't expand your space very much, and is unsafe to boot! I think this is the best.

This loft bed is designed with young adults in mind: their size and their needs. This is not planned for small children. I do not recommend loft beds for small children. In fact, the government regulations clearly state that no child under age six should be allowed on an upper bunk of any kind! They define an upper bunk as thirty inches or more above the floor. Although one of the chapter options is making bunk beds, they are two distinctly different designs, of different proportions. There is a child size, and an adult size. Please read, understand, and use good judgment.

The builder and the user must assume all risks associated with all phases of the construction and use of this do-it-yourself loft bed. Although the author has endeavored to write thorough and safe instructions, the author cannot supervise on-site. Furthermore, as the instructions progress beyond the basic structure, less is said about safety, in general. It is still important! I only assume that you have read it many times to get that far. I hope that you establish safe work habits from the beginning and maintain them.

Now you are beginning what may be your first DIY project, or at least the biggest to date. Good luck to you! The results are worth the effort. I think you have chosen the best because of the safety, durability, and way-cool accessories!

TABLE OF CONTENTS

Chapter 1   Building the Basic Bed Frame 1

Chapter 2   Let's Cut Some Wood! 7

Chapter 3   Major Sub-Assembly 13

Chapter 4   Surface Finish   17

Chapter 5   On-Site Assembly 19

Chapter 6   Bedside Table Accessory   23

Chapter 7   The Executive Desk Option   29

Chapter 8   The Transverse Desk 33

Chapter 9   Cable Up! 39

Chapter 10   Shelf Storage System   43

Chapter 11   Drawers and More 51

Chapter 12   Clothes Hanging I, II, and III 65

Chapter 13   Build it as a Bunk Bed   71

Chapter 14   More Resources. 79

Appendix A   Standards and Regulations   83

Appendix B   Specialty Vendors 83

CHAPTER ONE

BUILDING THE BASIC BED

To get started you must familiarize yourself with the options, and make your choices. You, the builder/user, will choose your own design parameters. For example; which mattress system will you use? Will you have modular furniture, or will you build it in place? Is there sufficient closet space? How about file storage? Books, papers, cds, electronic goods, etc. The following chapters will show you a lot of options for these categories and more. Breeze through the book first, check off which ideas appeal to you, and then you can home in on your final choices. In any case the basic bed frame is first on any list.

If you are starting from scratch, you will buy a standard size mattress and you will make the frame as dimensioned. On the other hand, if you are lofting an existing bed provided by a dormitory, chances are it has a flat steel frame with small tensioning springs. (Some manufacturers call this a link spring.) You will be fastening this steel frame to your home built wood frame. It is important to note that many of these steel frames are not a standard mattress size. If you are not positive of the length, just wait to cut all your wood rails to length on-site. These usually have conventional mattresses with compression springs. Either a plywood panel or wood slats can also support your mattress. I do not recommend using a box spring, or foundation, with your mattress on a loft bed. It adds nothing to the sleeping function and would be visually bulky, increasing the height almost a foot! Increasing the height decreases the headroom. You really do need the headroom.

There are a few different options for the headboard appearance. What I think of as a pillow stopper, is a plain board, purely functional. It has no decorative value beyond the color and grain of the wood. Whether you choose the 1 x 8 size or the 1 x 12 size, it should keep your pillow off the floor.

ARCHED HEADBOARD

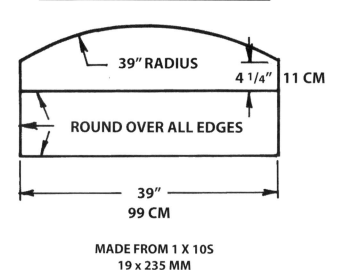

39" RADIUS

4 1/4" | 11 CM

ROUND OVER ALL EDGES

39"
99 CM

MADE FROM 1 X 10S
19 x 235 MM

RECURVE HEADBOARD

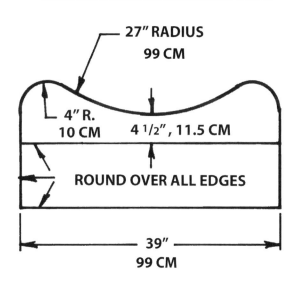

27" RADIUS
99 CM

4" R.
10 CM   4 1/2", 11.5 CM

ROUND OVER ALL EDGES

39"
99 CM

MADE FROM 1 X 10S
19 x 235 MM

A true headboard, on the other hand, is decorative. It displays the aesthetic sense of its maker. There are many classic furniture styles that can be emulated with the headboard shape. The real trick lies in choosing a shape that goes with or enhances the overall loft bed appearance. The few examples shown have a simple shape that doesn't clash. As a bonus; they are easily made by a beginning wood worker.

A couple more tools are needed to make either of these examples. A power saw to cut the curved outline, and a spoke shave plane to make it smooth. I like to cut them on a band saw, but a saber saw will work too. Once you have smoothed out the edges, round over everything and sand out uniformly smooth like the rest of the project.

I purchased a good quality laminated foam mattress. This came with arched hardwood springs (slats). It has proved quite satisfactory. This supplier can be found in the index in the back of the book. These mattresses come in two standard lengths; 75" and 79". If you are over six feet tall, buy the longer one. A few mattress manufacturers will also special order an 84" size for the really tall person. Since the quality of your mattress affects your sleep, your posture, and your health, it makes sense to buy a quality level you can live with.

Note the alternate foot rail design. It is a little easier to pass through.

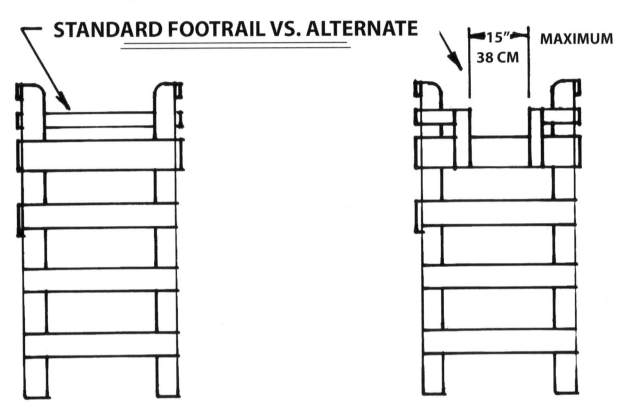

STANDARD FOOTRAIL VS. ALTERNATE

15" 38 CM MAXIMUM

Start by copying the material lists for each of the options you have chosen. Fasten these together so you end up with everything you need. Most of this will be heavy, bulky lumber and fasteners. It is not going to fit in a compact car. You can arrange for delivery, or you can bring it home yourself with a pickup, van or trailer.

You will need both hand tools and power tools to accomplish this project. Perhaps you already own some. Maybe a parent or friend will lend some of them to you. If you can't promote them somehow, you will have to buy them. Study the enclosed lists, and please don't neglect the safety gear. Now let's go shopping!

Basic Hand Tool Collection

Safety glasses , ear plugs , work gloves with non slip palms
2 – sharp pencils , durable tape measure at least 12' long
    (3.5 meter)
2 – speed squares, 1 large and 1 small
1 – hard rubber sanding block
1 – small putty knife or three-in-one
1 – finish hammer , 1– caulking gun
1 – utility knife , 1 – hand broom
1 – assortment of small drill bits and screw tips

Basic Safety Gear

1 – 25' extension cord with ground and at least 16 guage thickness (8 meters) long
1 – hard rubber splitter plug
1 – electric drill, preferably cordless
1 – 7¼" circular saw with a sharp carbide blade, 40 tooth,(185mm)

Power Tools

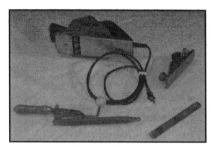

Planes and Rasps

1 – electric router with a ⅜ round over bit,(10mm)
1 – belt sander with medium or fine abrasive belt
2 – large spring clamps, for 3" material (80mm)
2 – folding sawhorses

10 – sheets of 100# sandpaper, production grade
1 – 12 ounce tube construction adhesive (.35liter)
6 – 1¼" course thread construction screws (3 cm)
1# – 2" course thread construction screws (5 cm)
1# – 2½" course thread construction screws (6.5 cm)
1# – 3" course thread construction screws (8 cm)
8 – ⁵/₁₆" x 4" lag screws (8mm x 10 cm)
8 – ⁵/₁₆" flat washers (8mm)
2 – ¼" wafer head screws (3 cm)
4' of ¼" flat loop chain (7mm x 1.2m)
4 – 11" zip ties (28 cm)

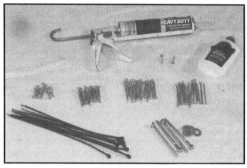

Misc. Fasteners

5 – 2 x 4 x 8' SPF (38 x 89 mm x 2.4 m)
3 – 2 x 8 x 8' SPF (38 x 184 mm x 2.4 m)
2 – 2 x 6 x 10' SPF (38 x 140 mm x 3 m)
4 – 2 x 6 x 8' SPF (38 x 140 mm x 2.4m)
2 – 2 x 2 x 8' SPF (38 x 38 mm x 2.4 m)
1 – 1 x 8 x 8' No. 2 pine (19 x 184 mm x 2.4 m)
1 – 1 x 6 x 8' No. 2 pine (19 x 140 mm x 1.8 m)
1 – 1 x 12 x 4' No. 1 pine (19 x 286 mm x 1.25 m)

If you chose to loft an existing steel bed platform (often called a link spring) the material list must be revised to accommodate this. For example, the 2 x 8 mattress rails can be eliminated. An additional 2 x 6 safety rail must be added in its place. Likewise; the center restrainer chain can be eliminated along with the zip ties. 1½" lag screws replace the 4" lag screws. The other fasteners remain the same. Substitute the following wood material list for the above.

6 – 2 x 4 x 8' SPF
1 – 2 x 8 x 8' SPF
2 – 2 x 6 x 10' SPF
1 – 1 x 8 x 8' #2 pine
1 – 1 x 6 x 8' #2 pine
1 – 1 x 12 x 4' #2 pine

Rounding over the sharp corners with a router really saves a lot of time. This can also be done with a block plane and sandpaper. Likewise, the belt sander is a huge time saver over hand sanding. Home built sawhorses can substitute for store bought. Substitutions, in essence, replace your time for expense. Some are a good trade, some are not, and some are equal. Obviously, these lists and my recommendations reflect my experience. They seem the wisest choice!

There are a few more tools required for some of the other chapter options; # 6 and #8 for example. Bear that in mind when you compile your shopping list. It is further assumed that you have a broom to sweep your work area and adequate light to work by. If not, promote a broom and a shop light too.

If you are buying your materials at a real lumber yard, the clerk prices your list, receives your payment, and arranges for the yard staff to fill your order. You generally receive their average quality material. They may even deliver at no additional charge.

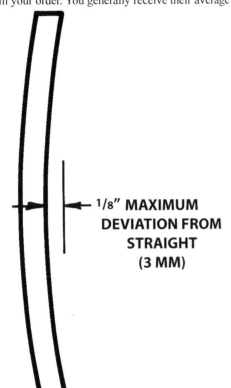

1/8″ MAXIMUM DEVIATION FROM STRAIGHT (3 MM)

If however, you shop at a home improvement center, you pick out your own material. The SPF designation means, construction grade spruce, pine, or fir. The #2 grade specification means at least #2! #1 is even better, and clear is better still. The better grade is more expensive. By sorting through the pile, you can usually find visually acceptable material in the grade specified. Remember: you are the quality control! Always try to get the best you can. Your lumber should be pretty straight and flat with no twist. Strive for 1/8″ (3mm) or less deviation from nominal. Less is better! You also want a fine grain structure, not the course grain of minimal "stud" grade. This stuff splits annoyingly inside a heated house. Remember: "just the good stuff" and "straight as a board". Small tight knots are ok (1/4"). Avoid larger and especially loose knots. Avoid wany edges (bark) splits, checks, and rough sawn. This will be your furniture, so get the best you can.

Once your order is assembled, you load it in your vehicle, secure it, and drive it home. I like bungee cords for this. They really make it fast and easy to secure long boards. They don't have knots to untie at the site, and I never have to cut them, unlike twine. I can reuse them over and over. Don't forget a red flag on any long boards. (They should have them at the gate.) My state says anything overhanging 2' (.6m) past the bumper needs a flag!

Use good work habits when lifting or carrying lumber. There are no bonus points for saving time if you strain your back or drop something on your foot. Use your legs for lifting, instead of your back. Keep the load close to your body. Try to imagine a short string connecting the board with your navel. If the center of gravity is at arm's length it just isn't graceful. Try to use leverage in your favor. Show good sense. Keep a clear walking path and a neat work space; no trippers!

Establish your work space. You will need a place to build your loft bed; someplace that dust, debris, noise and smell won't ruin. A garage stall, carport, or the corner of a basement, are about right. An actual workshop would be awesome! Your workspace will need good light to work by, electricity to run power tools, and ventilation. So long as you sweep up every work day, limit your noise to reasonable hours, and don't spoil anyone's prized possessions, temporary use should be doable! Once you agree to the conditions attached to the permission, stick to them. Most people will stay on your side if you hold up your end of the bargain. It is sometimes wiser to protect permanently stored items with tarps or plastic than moving them. After all, you are going to sweep up every work day right? Moving things always includes a risk of dropping, breaking, bumping, and damage. Besides, you don't need the space for a year, you just need it for a couple weeks. Be considerate with your noise and mess. Power tools can be extremely annoying to neighbors, so limit their hours. Many cities have noise ordinances restricting the hours you can work. Where I live, it is 7am to 10pm. (0700–2200). I wouldn't run a power saw or router at 9pm though,(2100). That wouldn't be a very good neighbor.

Try not to make enemies of your neighbors with visual offense either. If you make an eyesore within view of their most used window, they will react. Even if it is just temporary to you, to them it is ugly. If you are reasonable to other people, most will be reasonable back to you.

You will need a way to store your tools and supplies. Putting them back in one place, as you use them, really helps. You will lose less and stay safer. You will also waste less time looking for things. A large shelf or workbench is ideal. Drawers, cabinets, pegboard, toolboxes etc., will work, too. Whatever you have; stay with it for the duration.

Safety is not just about lifting and carrying. It is protecting all parts of your body from damage during all phases of work. It is usually easier to avoid damage than wearing it forevermore.

1. Wear safety glasses whenever you operate power tools, especially circular saws. Clean them often so you can actually see.
2. Use ear plugs around noisy things. You will hear better for it.
3. Wear a dust mask around dust, especially routing and sanding. I usually get the paper type with an exhaust valve for this.
4. Pickup or sweep aside debris and cut off pieces so you don't stumble on them.
5. Keep cords, unused lumber, etc. out of your walkway.

6. Follow the instructions on your power tools. Use them the way they were intended. That is how they work best.
7. Only use sharp blades. Whether it is a utility knife, block plane or circular saw. Dull blades require too much effort, lessen your control, and increase your risk of injury.
8. Use work gloves with non-slip palms for carrying and working with your lumber. Try to minimize the wear and tear on your hands. Not all blisters and splinters are inevitable.
9. Whatever you do, keep your fingers clear of blades and moving parts! If something gets in the way, turn off the motor and wait for the blade to stop. You can replace wood. You cannot undo an injury.

You really need some sawhorses for this project. They make it easier and safer. You will also get better results than working on the floor. The folding type are superior to the non-folding, as you can store them in a smaller space when you aren't using them. They are easier to transport too. Imagine sharing a pair with a friend to build their loft bed project! Whether you buy them ready made or build your own, there are a few essential guidelines to bear in mind.

1. You need them tall enough to keep your work piece within handy reach, sparing yourself back strain and fatigue.
2. You need large enough units to hold something large. The ladder frames you will build are 39" wide and 7' long. (1 meter x 2.2 meter)
3. You will need something sturdy enough to support the weight you will load them with.

I have reused my own folding sawhorses hundreds of times. I merely replace the sacrifice board when it gets too far gone. Notice how the board cantilevers past the end a few inches to support larger work pieces. A longer cantilever would make it unstable. These are plenty strong to support this amount of wood. They are widely available at lumber yards and home improvement stores.

Some pretty good sawhorses can be easily and cheaply made too. For this you trade off time for convenience. A couple hours of work could save you $50. The following drawings show a couple of examples, but by no means all. There is a rigid model and a folding model.

RIGID SAWHORSE

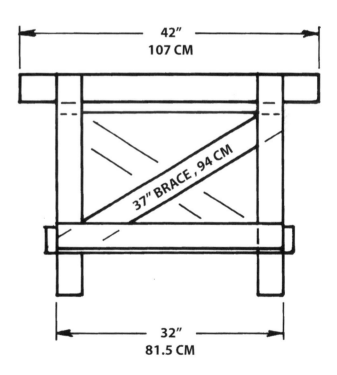

30"
76 CM

32"
81.5 CM

24" LG (61 CM)

6"
15 CM

24"
61 CM

BEVEL CUT LEG ENDS 17°

42"
107 CM

37" BRACE, 94 CM

32"
81.5 CM

MADE FROM 2 x 4s (38 x 89 MM)

FOLDING SAWHORSE

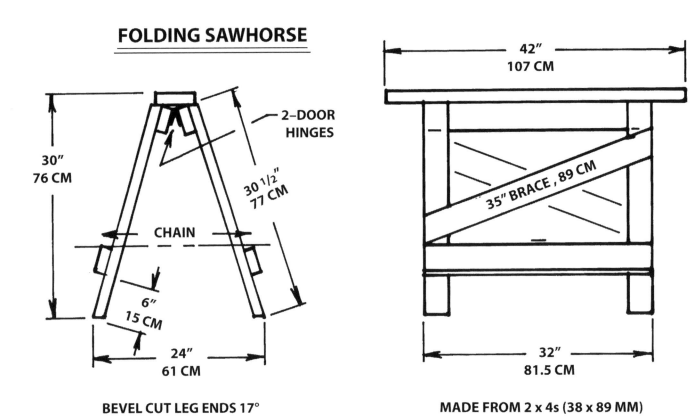

2-DOOR HINGES

30"
76 CM

30 1/2"
77 CM

CHAIN

6"
15 CM

24"
61 CM

42"
107 CM

35" BRACE, 89 CM

32"
81.5 CM

BEVEL CUT LEG ENDS 17°

MADE FROM 2 x 4s (38 x 89 MM)

The drawings are pretty self explanatory; but a few details have been purposely omitted to keep them legible. The saw horse sides must be squared before permanently attaching the diagonal braces. This means adjusting the shape so that it measures equally across both diagonals. The brace angle cuts are assumed to be scribed in place. Assembly is with construction adhesive and deck screws, both 2½" and 3" long (65 mm and 80 mm). The cantilevered sacrifice board on the folding model can only be fastened to one side: It wouldn't fold if you did both! Cantilevered ends can be cut shorter when the larger size is no longer needed. More care must be taken while using folding saw horses than the rigid type to avoid collapsing them under load. Never push or pull any folding saw horse while loaded! I recommend tacking a spreader board across their bottoms to prevent collapse with heavy loads. Light loads seem fine with out it. Use good sense and judgment, and you will be fine.

CHAPTER TWO

LET'S CUT SOME WOOD!

Begin by assembling everything you need in your work area. With all your wood on-site, your tools and your fasteners, and especially safety glasses, you are ready to start. Set up your saw horses first. String out your extension cord. Lay your first pieces of wood on top and begin.

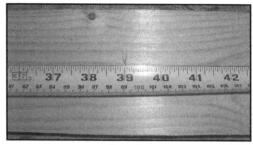
Measuring

I usually measure left to right because that is the way most tape measures read, with the numbers right side up. Hook it on the end of the board, pull it out far enough, and make your little v-mark pointing to the exact measurement. When you retract a tape measure, avoid snapping it in. The hook end breaks pretty easy. Instead; try to catch it, or cushion it with your finger. This trick will greatly prolong the useful life of a tape measure.

Next, line up your speed square with the point of your v-mark and draw across. Make an arrow or a check to indicate which side of the line you are intending the saw blade to cut. If I need four boards with the same measurement, I will mark and square all four before cutting. Next slide the speed square to the left a few inches, keeping the guide fence on the edge of your wood.

Be sure to put on your safety glasses and ear plugs before using power tools. Now position the leading edge of your circular saw bottom plate on the wood, with the left edge of the plate against the speed square. Slide both together to line up the saw blade exactly with the correct side of your pencil line. Hold the square firmly against the wood to prevent slipping, and make your cut. With just a little practice, you can make perfectly square cuts to any measurement specified. If you need to practice this technique a half dozen times to feel proficient, just allow your self some scrap wood and do it.

Saw Guide

You should preset the saw depth ¼" (6mm) beyond the thickness of the wood you are cutting. A visual comparison is much easier and faster than measuring this. The purpose is to clear the sawing debris out of the saw kerf. If you don't allow for this, you could experience the blade binding or burning, or even kickback.

Try to cantilever the scrap end past the saw horse, and keep the work piece fully supported whenever possible. That way you can work safely and efficiently alone. Always use a sharp saw blade. It makes a better cut, and it is easier.

Gang up for Efficiency

It is usually best to work through your list methodically, checking items off as you complete them. Occasionally I will resort to a masking tape sticker with the dimension written on it. This is when a project calls for several similar pieces, not identical in length. Another way to keep efficient is to stack your raw materials in one place and your finished cut pieces in another. These should be opposite sides of the work area and obvious.

The work habits you establish not only determine most of your workmanship, speed, and quality, but also your personal safety. You will determine the most important work area conditions.

FUTURE POWER SAW WITH ATTACHED HEADLIGHT

1. Be sure of adequate light. If you can't see your pencil line, how will you cut accurately or safely? Set up lights where and when you need them.

2. Move or pick up scrap cutoffs so you don't stumble on them . It isn't necessary to sweep after every cut, but you may have to brush off your next board to see your pencil line.

3. Position your work piece so you can reach it without straining. Over extending is a leading cause of injuries. Staying within your own range of balance and reach helps a lot. Remember the short string concept.
4. Try to arrange your electrical cords so they are not in the way, but have just enough slack. I usually like the cord routed behind me with a few loops of slack right there. You sure don't want the cord so tight you have to stretch it to finish the saw cut. Don't let the cord drop in the path of the spinning blade either.
5. Set the saw down out of the way between cuts. Whether to the side or behind, put it in the same place. That helps both speed and safety.
6. Don't use damaged tools. If your power tool has a bad cord, plug or switch; fix it right or replace it. Taping something up temporarily is just asking for trouble.
7. Never stand in water while using power tools. That includes wet grass and mud. Electrocution isn't funny.
8. Use eye protection and ear protection, please!

The basic loft bed consists of two end frames, plus two mattress rails, a spreader rail with angle brackets, four safety rails and a headboard. The following cutting list accounts for all the parts needed to build the bed frame using the standard length mattress. Please note; the headboard could be a 1 x 8 (19 x 184mm), a 1 x 12 (19 x 286mm), or two 1 x 10 (19 x 235mm), depending on your choice.

Note how the detail drawing of the mattress rail shows two different lengths. This accommodates the two standard mattress lengths; 75" and 79" (190 cm or 200cm). The spreader and safety rail lengths must also match lengths. 82" mattress rails get accompanying 82" rails and 86" mattress rails get 86" mates. In the interest of brevity, I have not repeated metric/English conversions ad infinitum on the same page.

The two end frames consist of:

- 4 – 2 x 6 x 77$^{1}/2$" from 8' boards (38 x 140mm x 197 cm) (2.4m)
- 2 – 2 x 8 x 39" from an 8' board (38 x 184mm x 99 cm) (2.4m)
- 6 – 2 x 6 x 39" from two – 10' boards,
  (38 x 140 mm x 99 cm (3m)

A	B	C	D
39"	77$^{1}/2$"	16"	64"
99 CM	197 CM	40.5 CM	162.5 CM

2 x 6 = 38 x 140 MM

2 x 8 = 38 x 184 MM

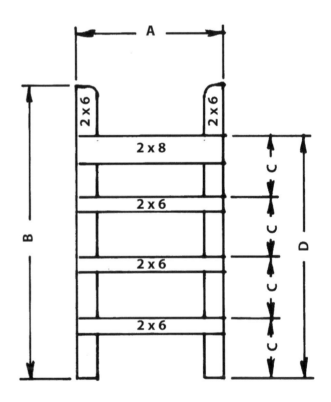

MATTRESS RAIL ASSEMBLY

The two mattress rails consist of :

- 2 – 2 x 8s from two – 8' boards, (38 x 184mm)
- 2 – 2 x 2s from two – 8' boards, (38 x 38 mm)

per drawing and mattress length choice.

MAKE FROM 2 x 8 (38 x 184 MM)
AND 2 x 2 CLEAT (38 x 38 MM)

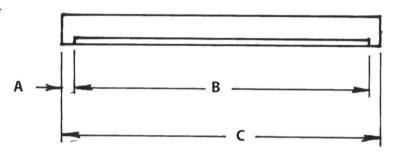

The spreader rail is:

- 1 – 1 x 8 x 82" from an 8" board (19 x 184 mm), equaling the mattress rail length.

	A	B	C
STANDARD LENGTH →	3"	76"	82"
	7.5 CM	193 CM	208 CM
LONG VERSION →	3"	80"	86"
	7.5 CM	203 CM	218.5 CM

The angle braces are :

- 2 – 1 x 6 x 51" from a 10' board; see drawing

ANGLE BRACE DETAIL

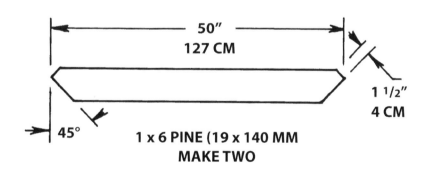

50"
127 CM

1 1/2"
4 CM

45°

1 x 6 PINE (19 x 140 MM
MAKE TWO

The safety rails are:

- 4 – 2 x 4s from four 8' boards (38 x 89 mm), equaling the mattress rail length.
- 1 – 2 x 4 x 39" foot rail, from 4' board (38 x 89 mm x 99 cm) (122 cm)

The headboard can be a

- 1 x 8 x 39" (19 x 184 mm x 99 cm), or
- 1 x 12 x 39" (19 x 286 mm x 99 cm), or
- 2 – 1 x 10 x 39" (19 x 235 mm x 99 cm), shaped per drawing in chapter one.

Follow this sequence to cut all the pieces to length.

First cut the two 2 x 8s to 82" long (or 86"), then the two 2 x 2s. Next; cut the 1 x 8 x 82" long (or 86"). Move these aside. Now put all your 2 x 4s and 2 x 6s on the saw horses, at least two pieces thick. Set the remaining 2 x 8 on top of this. Mark off the two 39" pieces. Block underneath it with your cutoff scraps, leaving a clear space in the cutting zone under your mark. Cut these and move them aside. Do the same for your 2 x 6 x 39" pieces. Move them to the finished pile. Move the scrap out of the way. Now mark and cut four of the 2 x 4s to 82" long. (or 86")Move them to the finished pile. Mark and cut the last four 2 x 6s to 77½" long, and move them. Next cut the headboard to length, and finally, make the two angle braces as shown in the drawing. When you have completed cutting all your parts to length, sweep up your work area.

The next phase is rounding over the edges. Rounding your edges now will prevent splinters in your hands later. The easiest, fastest way is with a router. If you can't promote a router; it can be done with a sharp block plane. Obviously the radius will end up much smaller. Some hand sanding will also be necessary. Set the plane blade depth about the thickness of heavy paper.

Hold the plane at an oblique angle and make a few swipes along each of the sharp wood edges. Try to make a smooth motion with even pressure. Long shavings are the proof of correct technique. A block plane is a small, one handed tool. A jack plane is really too big and unwieldy for this. Don't attempt this with a power plane. It is just not made for it. It could get ugly.

A router is ideal for rounding over edges. I like a ³/₈" radius (10 mm) carbide bit for this. The carbide edge lasts much longer than plain steel. A ½" radius (13 mm) is ok too. ¾" radius (19 mm) is over kill. Bigger bits require a bigger router motor to power them, and many woods tear out roughly with big bits. Don't substitute here.

Router Direction

When edge routing, look to see which side of the tool bit will cut while pushing and which while pulling. Pushing is better. Pulling is never recommended. See photo. You just don't have control of the tool when pulling. Control of your power tools equals quality and safety.

Always rout the end grain first, and then the long sides. This will produce far fewer tear outs and a better finished appearance. Set the tool depth using some scrap wood as a practice piece. The top corner of a round over bit should not contact.(See photo.) Set it slightly high. You will hand sand a little bit anyway. If you set it too deep, it will plow a groove and you will hand sand a lot!

Setting Router Depth

I suppose it is a moot point, but keep your fingers away from the router bit while it is on! It spins at 30,000. RPM! It can quickly make pate` of any flesh it contacts. If you run into a problem, turn it off and set it aside. I even unplug mine to change bits. I don't want to bump a switch and start it accidentally, with my fingers in the danger zone.

Routers produce a lot of fine airborne dust. It is wise to wear a dust mask when using them. Breathing problems are noticeably exacerbated by fine dust. Routers also make a piercing noise. You can protect your self with a pair of ear plugs. This is true of power sanders, too.

Once everything is rounded, you are ready to sand it all smooth. A belt sander is the magic word at this point. Make that end grain really fine. Take out all the mill marks. Clean off any dirt. Sand out the grade stamps, too, if you can. Use the fine grit belt. Scrub the caked dust

Way More than a Bed on Stilts

from the sanding belt often with a stiff brush.

An orbital sander is ok for end grain; but I don't recommend its use for the long exposed board faces. You might just see all those little circles (orbits) after varnishing. Hand sanding with a hard rubber block would be better for them. Go with the grain, not across it. Use long motions. Sand everything out uniformly with 100# production paper. Clean the caked on dust from the paper often. Change it when it becomes dull.

Brush off the dust often as you near completion of the sanding phase. It is easier to evaluate your progress on dust free wood. When everything looks and feels uniformly smooth, you are ready to begin assembly. Don't relax your standards just because you are tired or your hands hurt. Come back to it fresh from a rest and get it right. You will be glad you did for years to come.

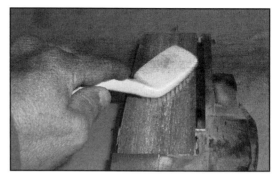

Cleaning Sanding Belt

C ongratulations. You are now ready to begin assembling the end frames and mattress rails.

Start by separating the four vertical supports from the already cut pile. These are 2 x 6s x 77½" long. (38 x 140 mm x 197 cm). Lay all four flat on the saw horses. Now hook your tape measure on the left end of your first board and pull it out to your first dimension. Mark it with a sharp pencil. Remember the v points exactly to the dimension measured. This time you must also mark a small x to the left of it. Repeat this for each dimension on the vertical support. When you finish marking the first 2 x 6, do the other three the same. Now, square across each of the v-marks.

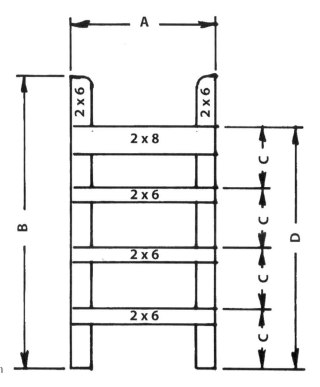

A	B	C	D
39"	77½"	16"	64"
99 CM	197 CM	40.5 CM	162.5 CM

2 x 6 = 38 x 140 MM

2 x 8 = 38 x 184 MM

Next; take out the 6 – 2 x 6 rungs (38 x 140 mm) and the 2 – 2 x 8 rungs (38 x 184 mm). Mark their hole locations as shown in the drawing. Now set up your electric drill with a sharp ³/₁₆" bit (5 mm). Make a hole through at every

HOLE LOCATIONS

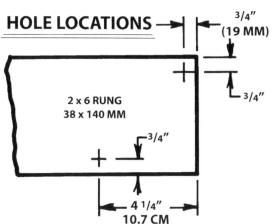

3/4" (19 MM)

2 x 6 RUNG
38 x 140 MM

3/4"

3/4"

4 1/4"
10.7 CM

mark. You should have two per end. Try to clear the sawdust debris from the hole, as you go. Just pull the drill out and wipe off the bit a couple times for each hole. This will help it drill better. Examine the back side of the board after drilling. If it is rough enough to prevent a tight joint, you must address that. Countersinking shallow is the quickest way. A few swipes across the grain with course sandpaper works too. I also countersink the face of any holes near the end of a board. This helps prevent splitting when driving the screws tight. Move the rungs to the new pile when you finish the holes.

Repeat Drilling Efficiently

Next take your 2 x 2s (38 x 38 mm) and put them on the saw horses. Starting 3" from each end (8 cm), lay out the hole locations on 8" centers, (20 cm). These must center the board. Drill these also with same ³/₁₆" bit, (5 mm). (You can skip this step if your mattress system chosen doesn't have the ledgers.) Otherwise move these to the new pile when done.

Now place one of the long 2 x 8s on the saw horses (38 x 184 mm). Sight down the long edges to determine which of them has the crown, or bulge. Put a little piece of masking tape near that edge. Position that board on the horses so that the crown mark is away from you and the best side is down. You will see that face once everything is assembled, so choose well for appearance! Now measure and mark 3" from each end (8 cm) at the edge nearest you.

Take one of your pre-drilled 2 x 2s, and run a ¼" (6 mm) bead of construction adhesive down the center of it. This is a side with holes in it. Preserve a couple inches glue free at each end. Try not to get it on your hands or clothes. Although it reduces with mineral spirits if wiped immediately, once it dries it must be worn off! Place that board glue side down, along the bottom edge of the 2 x 8. Align it to the end marks. Start some screws, flush the bottom edge with a scrap of wood, and drive in the screws. Work your way from one end to the other. Just snug the screws at first. After a few it will stay in position with less effort. When it is all screwed off, you can tighten them. You don't need to bury the screw head, and don't split the 2 x 2 at the ends either. Repeat this process for the other 2 x 8 and 2 x 2. When both mattress rails are assembled, move them out of the way. Clear out your working space. That includes the saw horses.

MATTRESS RAIL ASSEMBLY

MAKE FROM 2 x 8 (38 x 184 MM) AND 2 x 2 CLEAT (38 x 38 MM)

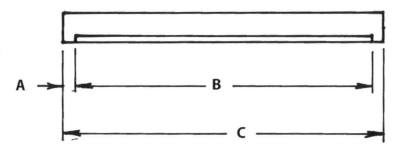

	A	B	C
STANDARD LENGTH →	3"	76"	82"
	7.5 CM	193 CM	208 CM
LONG VERSION →	3"	80"	86"
	7.5 CM	203 CM	218.5 CM

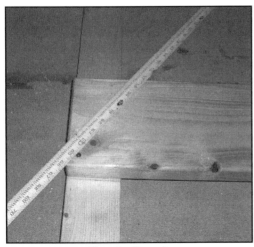

Measuring Diagonals

Start assembling the end frames by placing two of the vertical supports on the floor, with the marks up. Position the bottom ends against a wall, about three feet apart, (1 meter). (If you don't have a wall to use as a reference, you can use another board to align them.) Now get one of your 2 x 6 rungs (38 x 140 mm) for your lowest mark, and a 2 x 8 rung (38 x 184 mm) for your highest mark. Start one of the 2½" screws (65 mm) in each end of each rung. Apply the construction adhesive in a circular pattern within the highest and lowest pencil marks of your vertical supports. See photo. Do all four glue sites and release the dispensing pressure. Set it aside. Now put your first two rungs in position covering the adhesive. Hold it on the marks and flush the outside edge. Drive the screw in snug. Repeat this procedure for the other end of the rung on the other vertical support. When that is screwed snug, fasten the top rung (2 x 8) in the same way.

Adhesive Circle within Marks

You should now have a loose parallelogram. Hook your tape measure on the corner of the bottom rung, and measure diagonally across to the top rung. See drawing. Repeat this for the opposite diagonal. A square frame will be exactly the same across both diagonal directions. Adjust the shape to make them the same. If you keep the bottom ends firmly against the wall, you only need to warp the frame's top one way or the other. When it is perfect, tighten one of the screws and re-check. If it still looks right; tighten the other three screws. Re-check again. If it is all good, put your other screws in, sinking them tight. If you made it square this far, it will always be square. The glue and screws will hold it. When you have applied the adhesive, you must work fast. Break time will come and go with out notice during assembly. Take your other two rungs (2 x 6s) and attach them the same way.

SQUARING

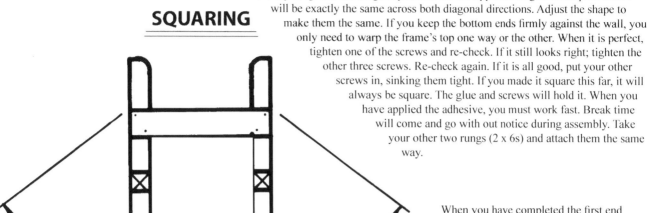

When you have completed the first end frame, move it out of the way, and begin the second one. You will notice the weight is beginning to add up. Practice good lifting and moving habits. Keep you hands far apart on the assembly for control and grace. Always try to keep the weight, or center of gravity,

Securing a Rung

close to your body. Whenever possible; tip it, rotate it, walk it on its own corners, etc., to spare your body bearing it. Using leverage and grace to your advantage can keep you injury free for your entire life. That is wisdom.

Give the glue an hour or so to harden up. Carefully scrape or gouge off any excess that has squeezed out of the joints. Touch up with sand paper now if you need to. A little mineral spirits on a rag can clean up a glue smear that is still liquid or gooey.

Now is the time to decide about wood putty. Yes or no? Are there any voids, splits, cracks, or open knots? If you use plastic wood filler, or putty, make sure it says pine! You would like the same color! Squeeze the wood filler into the voids at this time. Across the gap seems to work best. Wait for it to dry and sand it smooth. You are the quality control person. Personally, I accept hairline cracks as is, but if the cracks are wide enough to see as a dark line from three or four feet away, I will putty them. When this detail is done, you are ready to begin surface finish.

CHAPTER FOUR

SURFACE FINISH

Y ou did it! You got this far. You're cruisin'! Now the project really starts to look like something. Finishing the surface is visually rewarding. I hope you sanded everything out to the same consistency. A couple hours of effort, in the sanding phase, could make the difference to your overall satisfaction in this project.

I recommend a natural appearance, with spar varnish, or polyurethane to protect it. In my opinion, pine looks best unstained and unpainted. (Spruce, fir, maple, birch, and other blonde woods too.)

I will include directions for some other finishing options towards the end of the chapter.

Some colleges require that your home built loft bed either be finished with fire retardant paint, or you must attach a fire extinguisher to it. Fire retardant paint,(intumescent) is a product that prevents fires from spreading. It could save your life! I don't see it competing on appearance sake, though. It is formulated for just one purpose. If smoking, candles (open flame), and hazardous wiring are the worst fire hazards, then eliminating those risks, and keeping a fire extinguisher handy, should minimize the fire danger. (By the way, the mattress and bedding should also comply with fire safety regulations.)

The surface finishing phase really begins by cleaning the dust out of the work area, as best you can. Sweep the walls down too! You don't want that dust settling into your wet varnish. You will still need the saw horses (dust free of course). And ventilation is even more important now than it was for assembling. You will also need to assemble the necessary tools and supplies for finishing.

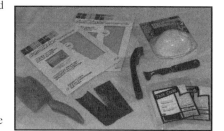
Finishing Supplies

Various Sanders

1. Dozen sheets of fine sandpaper (180#)
2. A few dust masks
3. A hand broom for dusting
4. Half dozen tack rags
5. Stiff putty knife/scraper/or three-in-one
6. 2½" (65 mm) wide varnish brush (china bristle)
7. 1 quart of mineral spirits (1 liter)
8. Clean, empty soup can or similar
9. 1 quart of quick dry sanding sealer (1 liter)
10. 1 quart of spar varnish, satin sheen (1 liter)
11. A few pairs of cheap surgical gloves

Varnishing Supplies

When your work piece(s) is smooth enough, dust it off with the hand broom. Next unfold one of the tack rags, and wipe off all the wood again. There is some rotating and refolding involved. You are trying to get the last of the dust here.

Now open the can of sanding sealer. Stir in any solids, until completely dissolved. Do not shake it! Brush on a thin coat of sealer. I get my best results when the work piece is lying flat, as on a sawhorse. The brushing is just as easy with the wood leaning up against a wall, but many more drips and runs happen. I think you have more control of the thickness you are applying that way.

When the sealer is dry enough, according to the directions, carefully turn the work piece over and prepare the other side. Scrape off any runs, drips, and goobers with the stiff putty knife. Touch up sanding if needed. Brush off the dust, Wipe it down with the tack rag, and apply sanding sealer to the second side. The exposed end grain will probably need a second coat of sealer, especially rungs.

In between applications I store the varnish brush in the soup can with an inch or so of mineral spirits. When I need the brush again; I just squeeze out the excess liquid on the edge of the can, and then "paint" it dry on some scrap cardboard or rags.

Once the sealer is dry, you must sand it with the fine sand paper. Use 180# for this. Start by cutting the sheet of sand paper in half, and then fold each of those in thirds. Hold it with your hand now instead of the block. Change the paper sides as it gets dull or filled. You are really not removing much material at this stage, just making it smoother. The sealer will cause a lot of the fine wood fibers to stand on end. It also fills in and seals the porous areas. As you sand, your hand will feel it getting smoother, and your eyes will see it turning a milky color of fine dust. Be sure to scrape any runs or drips with the putty knife. Make it all the same consistency. Brush off the dust and wipe it down carefully with a tack rag.

Now you should open the can of spar varnish. Carefully stir in any solids from the bottom of your varnish. If it is a new can, this could take several minutes. If it is an old can you might find a thick skin on top of the liquid. Cut it out and throw that part away. The skin forms when the can lid doesn't seal tight. Just clean the groove that receives the lid before resealing. Never shake varnish, only stir it. The bubbles that form will dry on your wood!

Clean and dry your brush before using it. Pull out any loose bristles. It can be really annoying to have them shed on your freshly varnished surface. Apply a uniformly thin coat of varnish to the flat surfaces, edges, and ends. Try to keep the work room dust free now. Sweep up between applications. Damp mop if you need to. You don't want dust landing in your wet varnish. Although it can be sanded smooth again, sanding is harder work than just avoiding the problem. When your work piece is dry, turn it over. Prepare and varnish the other side as before. It should be looking fine now. All surfaces and edges need at least one coat of varnish and a coat of sanding sealer. Top edges of rungs need two. They will receive more wear. Any other wear surfaces should get more varnish coats too. (Bed side table, book shelf, desk top, etc..)

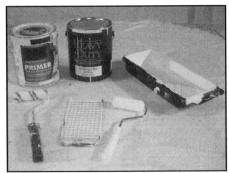

Painting Supplies

If you chose to stain or dye the wood, that is another step before the sealer is applied. There is no problem with shaking up stain. Stirring works, too. Just remember that the pigment solids must be completely dissolved before applying the stain. If not, the end of the can may be a lot darker than the beginning of the can. You brush it on your wood thick, and wait a few minutes, then wipe it off with clean rags or wiping pad.

The longer you wait before wiping, the darker your wood will become. Think: rate of absorbtion. Strive for a fairly uniform color tone. Let the grain figuring do the rest. It is critical to stain both sides before applying sealer! No stain absorbs through the sealer. You sure don't want any bare spots showing! Sand with fine paper between sealer/varnish coats. If you get some white wood showing with the fine sanding, just reapply some stain to the affected area. Let it dry and wipe it. Succeeding varnish coats can be sanded with even finer paper to produce an even finer finish, like 220#.

If you chose to paint your loft bed project, you must buy primer and paint instead of sealer and varnish. You will also need a better grade of brush and a mini-roller. The cloth fiber rollers are fine for applying the primer, but you will need the rounded end foam roller to paint with. The mini-roller applies much faster than a brush. It doesn't take near as much practice to achieve the desired finish either.

Water based primer works fine on most wood, but it just doesn't seem to hide the knots. They require two coats of the stinky stuff, either an oil based product or the pigmented shellac. When the primer is dry, per instructions, you sand it with fine paper between coats. Dust it off and tack it off good before applying your paint.

I would use a latex semi-gloss enamel paint for this, if you must paint. Two thin coats are much more durable than one thick one. One great thing about latex paint, versus oil base, or alkyd; is the ease of clean up. Soggy rollers can be wrapped up tight in a plastic bag and kept for days. Brushes can be combed and rinsed in a laundry tub. It takes about five minutes! You just keep working it until no more color comes out.

Feel free to personalize your loft bed. It is yours! Stencilling, lettering, stickers, pictures etc. Good luck and enjoy your project.

Let the surface finish cure out bone hard before transporting to the final assembly point. I know I'm repeating myself here, but dry to the touch is not the same as cured through. The finish is soft underneath for awhile and easily marred by rough handling. Patience really is a virtue. So just do something else for a couple of days while you wait: like building one of those way cool accessory options!

CHAPTER FIVE

ON-SITE ASSEMBLY

Once the finish is cured hard, you should pre-drill your wooden parts, as much as possible, at your work area. This will keep the sawdust out of your dorm room. Measure, mark, and drill all the holes detailed in the drawing for the mattress rails. Take note; there are two sizes of holes there. Repeat for both mattress rails. Mark and drill the two holes on both ends of the mattress ledger as well. Mark and drill the ends of the spreader rail and the safety rails also. Pre-drill the angle braces too. This completes the prefabrication phase. If you had drilled before the surface finish was applied, the varnish would have run through the holes, and formed even more runs, drips, and goobers. Scheduling the hole drilling at this point saves you the work of scraping and sanding those. (It also improves the quality.)

The next step is to transport everything to its final destination. Whether you are going to a college dormitory, a rented apartment in a distant city, or just across town, you will need to use a vehicle of adequate size and capacity to transport your belongings. Perhaps a pickup truck, or full size van (minus the seats), or maybe a trailer of some kind will work for you. Perhaps a moving van is in the picture. Bear in mind that the greater the distance traveled, the fewer trips you will want to make. Arranging a large enough vehicle could save you time and trips.

I recommend bundling similar size wood parts together. For example; all four safety rails and the spreader rail together. Put both mattress rails together. Since weight is an issue for most people, don't make the bundles so large or heavy that an average person can't carry them. Blue masking tape is good for bundling. So is shrink wrap or twine. (Duct tape leaves too much residue.)

When you get to loading the vehicle, try to put the big things in first, and then pack the smaller things around them. It is a good idea to protect your furniture with mover's blankets, or old rugs, cardboard, etc. Wedge things in tight and tie them off to prevent load shifting. It can, and does, happen during the drive. Also try to load in such a way that your loft bed can be one of the first things out.

Completed Assembly with Accessories

Once you arrive at your new lodgings, bring in and erect your loft bed first. You need some empty space for this. Carry all the components to your new room. Put the end frames where the bed will go, and set the rails nearby. You should remove their bundling tape now. Don't crowd yourself at this point. Leave any other components, furniture, or luggage, well out of the way until this is assembled. You also need a helper for assembly, just like you did for moving. While one person holds, the other builds. There is some lifting and moving involved, too. The following assembly instructions are for the basic loft bed design from chapter one. If your application doesn't have mattress rails, or reuses an existing metal bed spring platform, you will need to read the special instructions at the end of this chapter.

Start with your end frames standing on edge, with the rung sides together, and their feet touching the wall. See photo. While one person holds the frames up, the other measures and marks the "top" edge of both vertical supports. The practical way is to hold a frame against each side of their body. The spreader is the first piece you attach to them. Hold one end on its marks and flush with the edge, and secure with a 2" (50 mm) course thread screw. Don't sink it! Just snug it for now. Now do the other end. While one person holds up the frame, with the board attached, the other person moves the second frame over to its position at the other end of the spreader. Hold it on the marks and flush with the edge and put a screw in that end. Use the bottom corner hole in both ends.

The second piece is the top safety rail. Put it in its place, making the ends and top edges flush. Secure it with a 3" (80 mm) screw in each end. Again, just snug it for now. Next, take one of the angle braces and hold it to the appropriate marks on the vertical support. Fasten this with 2" (50 mm) screws. If it is on the marks and flush, this can be screwed tight, all three holes. See photo. Notice how the other end of the angle brace lays loose on top of the spreader for now. Attach the other angle brace the same way.

The top edge of your beginning frame assembly should be a loose parallelogram now. One person must still hold it up. Measure the diagonals for squareness. Keep both frame feet tight to the wall for this. Your tape measure should be hooked from the bottom corners of the end frames, and measures to the top corners of the safety rail. If the screws were only tightened to "snug", the vertical supports are easily pushed or pulled to adjust the shape. When the diagonal measurements are exactly equal, the frame is square. Fasten an angle brace to the spreader with a 1¼" (30 mm) screw. Recheck your measurement. If it is still good, attach the other brace to the spreader. Recheck for square again. Back up and adjust if necessary. When you are satisfied, fill in all the missing screws per assembly drawing below, and tighten everything. Both braces should also be thru-bolted to the spreader rail. Use the hole location nearest the upper brace tip for this. Secure with a ¼" x 2" round head bolt, (6mm x 50 mm), 2 flat washers, and a lock nut. These things are crucial to having a sturdy and durable loft bed.

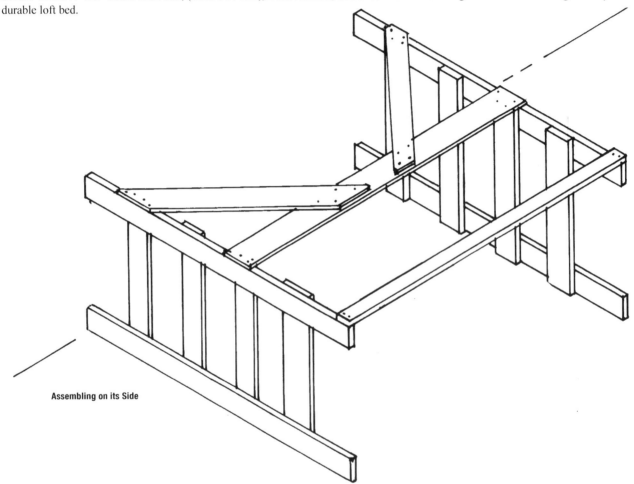

Assembling on its Side

You should put the mattress rail in place next. Be sure the 2 x 2 ledger is oriented down and towards the feet. See drawing. Make it fit tight to each end and secure with 3" (80 mm) screws. Next put the interim safety rail in place. Hold to its marks and fasten with 3" screws. Put in the last two screws in the top rail, and tighten up everything. It should stand up with out help now.

Next drill the pilot holes for the lag screws. These should be ³⁄₁₆" (5 mm) diameter. These must be drilled with the mattress rail in place. (Each mattress rail has two clearance holes on each end.) One goes into the vertical support, and one goes into the rung. These help the lags start, or "bite", without splitting the wood. Drive the lags in with your wrench. Don't forget the flat washers. Snug them sufficiently so the lag and washer are just starting to crush the wood.

Now that the back side is built you are ready to tip it up. This takes two people. With one person grasping each end frame, drag the entire assembly back a few feet from the wall. Lift and tip it up together. You must work together and talk together for this so that the effort is shared equally. When the frame is standing vertical on its own feet, you can attach the remaining rails.

Measure and mark the front edge of the vertical supports for the rail locations. See drawing. Drive an eight penny framing nail (60 mm) just touching the bottom of the line for the mattress rail. Now hoist the mattress rail into place, and rest it on the temporary nails. With one person holding it, the other person fastens it with more 3" (80 mm) screws. Put in one high, then one low, then the other end. Fill in all the screws. Strive to make the ends fit tight together. Then drill the 3/16" (5 mm) pilot holes for the lag screws on this side. Drive in those last lag screws with your wrench. Carefully pull the temporary nails (cushioning your wood) and apply nails for the top rail. Put the top rail in place, hold the ends and the top edge flush and secure with more 3" screws. Repeat this process for the interim rail. Make sure every hole has a screw in it and every screw is tight.

Finally, attach your headboard on the end of your choice. Fasten with more 2" (50 mm) screws. With that done, you are ready for the bed slats and mattress. If you are using the prefabricated wooden spring slat assembly, restrain the ends from movement by securing both sides of both ends with zip ties through the ledger holes and wrapping the last slat. This should prevent either end of the spring slat assembly from creeping away from the top rung. That creeping could potentially create a void, or space large enough to step through, or even entrap a body part.

If you are making your own bed slats, they should be rounded on all the long edges. Both ends should be drilled through and screwed to the mattress ledger as well. Space them about 1 1/2" (38 mm) apart. Keep the spacing uniform. The restrainer chain should be added now. This is fastened to the bottom side of the mattress rails, approximately center span. Measure and mark the centers, secure with the wafer head screws. Hold the chain about 1/2" (1 cm) in from the outside edge of the 2 x 8. This chain will prevent ledger spread. Though I have never heard of 2 x 8s bowing outward that much, if they did; part of the spring slat assembly could drop down, and scare the heck out of you!

Now would be a good time to install any other components you have built. When you are ready; lift the entire assembly over to its final, user, position. Hopefully you were close.

Congratulations, you did it! It is built now. You da' man! (Or woman.) Just finish moving your belongings and you are all set for the semester. If you have two or more of the accessory options: you have the coolest loft on campus!

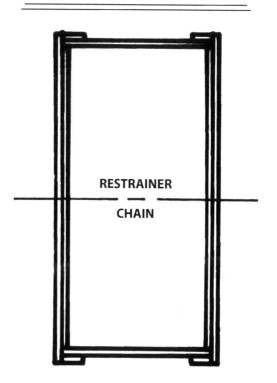

BOTTOM VIEW
MATTRESS PLATFORM

RESTRAINER
CHAIN

SPECIAL INSTRUCTIONS FOR USING A LINK SPRING

The existing metal bed spring platform is attached to the end frames with lag screws. You should need eight of them, plus flat washers. Get 5/16" x 1 1/2" long (8 mm x 38 mm). A socket wrench with ratchet is the best way to torque them in.

You will start with one end frame and the platform. Plan it so no metal flange hangs below the 2 x 8 top rung. Measure the hole spread dimensions, and transfer these to the 2 x 8. Pre-drill 3/16" (6 mm) pilot holes in the wood at the marks. Hold the frame and the platform together and lag them solid. If you do one high and one near the floor, it will stand up unaided. Go ahead and make them tight. Now you can measure, drill and attach the other end frame to the platform. Go ahead and put in all the lag screws it will hold.

Measure the total length of the metal platform, outside to outside. Add six inches to that. The new figure is your correct rail length. Cut them all.

Now lay out the "top" edge of the vertical supports for the rail locations. See drawing. The next step is to attach the spreader rail on its marks, then the angle braces, and the top rail. Square it up, brace it and secure with plenty of screws as before. There is one additional safety rail needed for use with the metal platform. The 2 x 6 (38 x 140 mm) replaces the 2 x 8 rail. The top of this rail should meet the top of the 2 x 8 rung. Since the mattress edge is soft, part of your body could squeeze under the other rails, with out it. The rest is the same as the standard design.

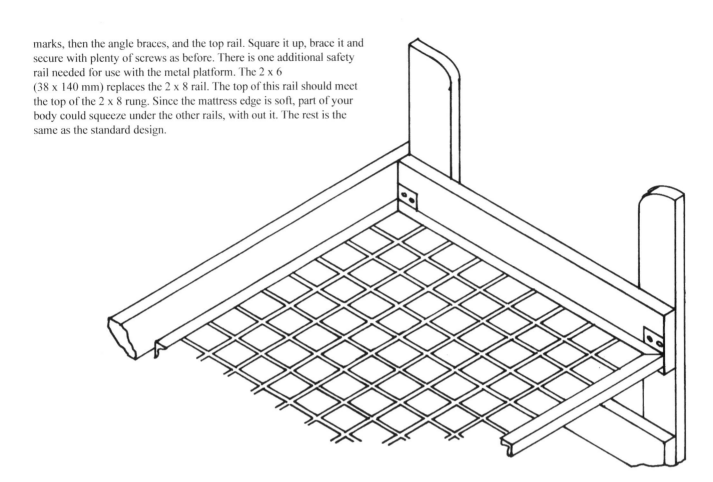

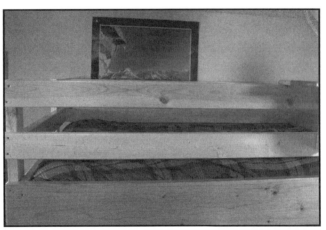

Double Guard Rails

Way More than a Bed on Stilts

CHAPTER SIX

BED SIDE TABLE ACCESSORY

This accessory is actually an attached shelf. It is meant to hold the typical personal goods used at the bed side. For example: clock-radio, telephone, water glass, oscillating fan, etc. Plenty of people seem to survive dorm life with only a clip on fan, but this is a lot better. This rocks! This is big enough, and close enough. The cleat helps prevents drop-offs of valuables. This accessory really works well!

Some really tall (and inattentive) people might find this a head banger. I recommend rounding and smoothing all the edges and corners. That should prevent the drawing of blood from any accidental encounter. Some people will put reflective hazard tape on any head high obstacles, including the mattress rail. (Is that a bit much)? I feel that if you use sense and good judgment, this item will serve you well. This is not designed to support your body weight. Don't climb on it or do pull-ups from it. Everything has its limitations. This is a bedside table. It works well for that.

There is not a lot of lumber required to make this piece, but there are a couple of different tools and techniques involved. The component parts have radiused ends. Ideally, you

BEDSIDE TABLE

would use a bandsaw to cut these (a large stationary power tool). If unavailable, perhaps you could borrow a saber saw (a hand held power tool). Barring that, you might do it with a coping saw (a hand tool). The saw marks are then smoothed from the curved portion of your wood with a spoke shave plane. Rounding over and sanding finishes the shaping process.

You will need a 1 x 12 x 4' (19 x 286 mm x 1.25 m), and a 2 x 10 x 6' (38 x 235 mm x 2 m), and a 1 x 1 x 3' (19 x 19 mm x 1 m). Some construction adhesive and some wood glue are also needed, plus some fasteners. You need a dozen 3" (80 mm) deck screws, four 2" (50 mm) deck screws, six 4d (40 mm) finish nails and six 1 ¼" (30 mm) brads.

Start by cutting the 1 x 12 to 42" (107 cm) length. As always, try to make your cut nice and square and clean. Draw your radiuses on both ends. In the process, you must pick the nicer side. Make a little pencil mark or attach a little piece of masking tape or something to indicate the "A" side, or top. The plan calls for a six inch radius on the ends. You can plot their centers with your 12" (30 cm) square, and scribe the quarter circumference with a compass. Or you could just draw around a five gallon bucket, large mixing bowl, whatever you have. The exact radius measurement isn't crucial; making it look good is.

Bedside Table Installed

Next, scribe the radius on both ends of your 2 x 10 (38 x 235 mm). You will have a total of four radius cuts to make, whichever of the saws you use. Carefully cut them out to the line and not over. Touch up any roughness and saw marks with a spoke shave plane. See photo. Next, you must sand it smooth, all the way around the curve and both tangents. The belt sander works great for this, but the hard rubber block will do it too.

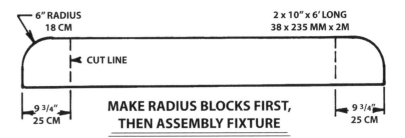

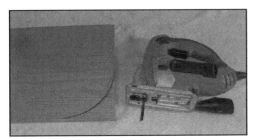

Cutting a Radius

Once you are satisfied with the curves, you must cut the ends off the 2 x 10. Measure back 9¾" (25 cm) from each end, square it and cut it. Having that extra material during the "curve" procedure makes it easier. Try not to get out of sequence. These need to be good, square, clean cuts. Touch them up with a plane and sander if you need to.

Next bring out your router with the round over bit still attached. The 1 x 12 (19 x 286 mm) gets the treatment on all edges and both sides. Rout it slowly on curves and in the direction shown. See photo. Note how the 2 x 10 (38 x 235 mm) radius blocks do not get their top edges rounded. All other edges should be. The 1 x 1 (19 x 19 mm) cleat also requires rounding. You should hold it to your work surface with some spring clamps. Lay some 1 x material next to it to support the router base as you machine the edges. Move the spring clamps as you go. Remember to keep your fingers clear!

Shaping a Radius Block

With the top edges rounded, cut the 1 x 1 to length. Now round both ends with a rasp and sandpaper. Then sand out everything uniformly. Remove any mill marks, scratches, etc. Sanding smooth is the step that makes your reputation. All of it should feel smooth to your hand when you finish.

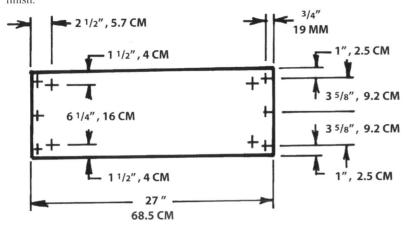

**REAR SPREADER FOR
ASSEMBLY FIXTURE
REQUIRES TWO BLOCKS ALSO**

To begin assembly, you will measure, mark, cut and pre-drill the 2 x 10 cut off piece. This will become an assembly fixture to facilitate assembling the three rounded pieces. Without it, everything wants to rock and tip while you pound in your nails. Cut the 2 x 10 scrap into three pieces, as per drawing, and assemble with screws. Drill the extra holes in it too. Add the 1 x 3 (19 x 70 mm) cleat to the upper rear edge, per drawing. That's it. It is a pretty simple fixture.

ASSEMBLY FIXTURE

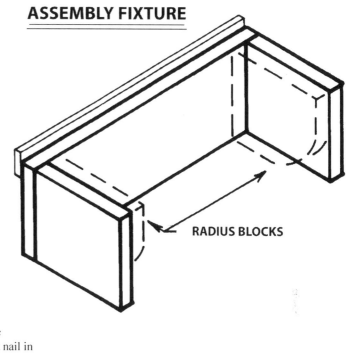

Next, fasten the two radius blocks to the fixture with more 3" (80 mm) screws. See drawing.

Next you must measure and mark the overhang distance for both ends on the rear edge of the 1 x 12. Run a ¼" (6 mm) bead of construction adhesive along their top edges of the blocks. Do not apply adhesive to any part of the fixture.

Next, layout the nail locations on the top side of the 1 x 12. Start some six penny finish nails at each location. Carefully lay the 1 x 12 on top of the 2 x 10s as shown in photograph. Do not slide it, or move it, once it makes contact with the adhesive. Try to set it down in the correct position. Flush the long straight edge to the temporary spreader using the 1 x 3 cleat. Align the two edge marks with their corresponding marks on the spreader. Temporarily secure to the fixture with two 2" screws, far apart. Now drive the first nail in most of the way, leaving about ¼" sticking out. (The two rear nails, nearest the spreader, should be first and second.) Recheck your edge and marks and drive your second nail, into the second block. Stop well short of flush.

RADIUS BLOCKS

TOP VIEW

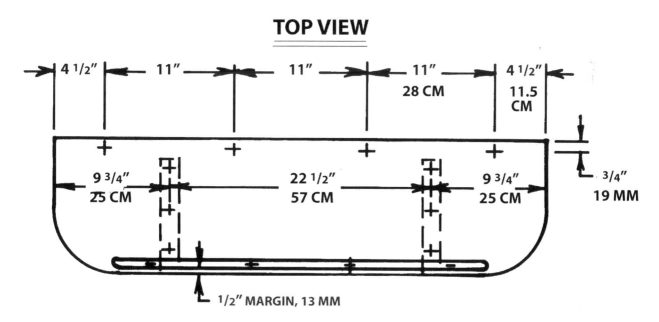

Nail the outer edge of the 1 x 12, making sure the radius blocks are on their marks. Nail first one and then the other. Don't sink them yet. Re-check the assembly for accuracy. It should be looking like the drawing and the photos. If it is ok, go ahead and sink your nails with a nail set. Try not to dimple the wood surface. You might as well drive the third nail (middle) into the block and sink it, too (both blocks).

If the nailing is crooked or bending or otherwise poor quality, just pull them out with the hammer claws. Be sure to protect the wood surface with a scrap. Pulling can mar the surface as bad as pounding. Start a new nail near the old location. Avoid knots!

Next start some brads in the 1 x 1 as shown in the drawing. Keep them straight up and vertical. Next lay the 1 x 1 in its assembly position, see photo. Make a few light pencil marks to assist you here. Run a light bead of wood glue along the bottom edge of the 1 x 1. Carefully place the 1 x 1 on its marks. No sliding! Hold it with your spring clamps, and drive in the brad nearest the end, and then the one on the opposite end.

FRONT VIEW

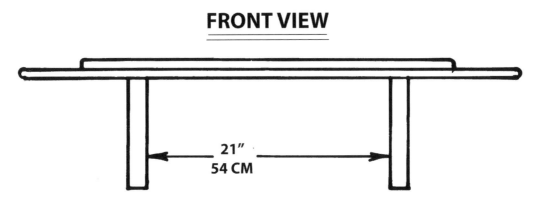

21"
54 CM

Remove the two screws holding the 1 x 12 top to the fixture now, and the screws holding the radius blocks. Carefully lift the assembly out of the fixture, and turn it so that the square blocks can support the mid span nails for the 1 x 1 cleat. Reposition the fixture relative to the assembly, as you go, so that a square block bears under the 1 x 12 for every brad nail you fasten the cleat with. Drive all your brads. Sink them carefully with a nail set. That should finish the need for the fixture.

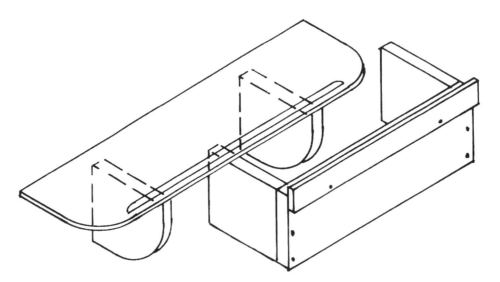

If you used too much glue or adhesive, now is the time to deal with it. Wood glue cleans up with water, or better yet a damp rag. Try not to saturate your wood. It must be bone dry before sealing it. Gooey construction adhesive can be wiped off with mineral spirits on a rag. If it is hard, you must scrape and sand.

Apply the plastic wood putty to the nail holes now. Squeeze it in any voids with your putty knife/scraper. When it is completely dry (an hour or more), take some sandpaper to it. Smooth out any wood putty, rough grain, remove pencil marks etc. Make it all good. After all you are creating furniture here!

When you are ready, brush any dust off the top, rub it well with a tack rag, and apply a coat of sanding sealer. Try to clean any excess running over the edges to the bottom side while it is still liquid. When this is dry, according to the directions, lightly sand it with your fine sandpaper. Sweep it off, tack it off, and apply a thin even coat of spar varnish. Go very thin on the edges, don't let it run over if you can help it. Wait the appropriate time, and repeat the sanding, dusting, tacking, and reapplying more varnish. The top surface will take more abuse, so more varnish coats are justified.

When the top is quite dry, flip the assembly over and start on the bottom side. Touch up any sanding (and scraping) as necessary. Brush off the dust, tack it good and apply the sanding sealer. When this is dry, lightly sand it, dust it off, tack it off, and apply the spar varnish. Pay close attention to your edges. You don't want any runs, drips, or goobers to form there. Everything about this piece is at eye level and noticeable. When the surface finish is satisfactory and dried bone hard, you are ready to install.

MOUNTING HOLES

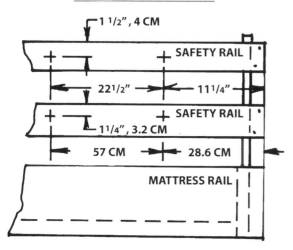

Lay out the four mounting holes in the top surface, as shown in the previous detail drawing. Pre-drill them with a $^3/_{16}$" (5 mm) bit, and countersink shallow. Next place the side table assembly in the desired position along the safety rails. I prefer all the way to the headboard, but some people like a centered location. It is your project, and your bed. You choose. Hold it tight to the safety rails and secure it with the 2" (50 mm) screws, down through the top. I highly recommend a 6' (2 m) stepladder for this, and a cordless drill with a screwdriver bit, too. Next you must drill through both safety rails into the end grain of both radius blocks. (Realistically, you must climb up on top of the bed for this.) Finally, drive a 3" (80 mm) screw into each of those holes. When all four are sunk flush, installation is complete.

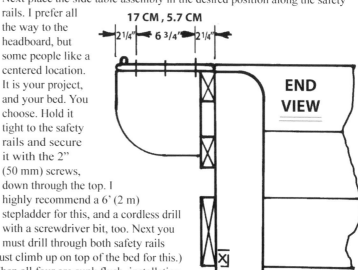

You now have a great place for your fan, clock radio, whatever you want. This is already better than any store bought loft bed and this is just your first accessory! Enjoy it and be proud!

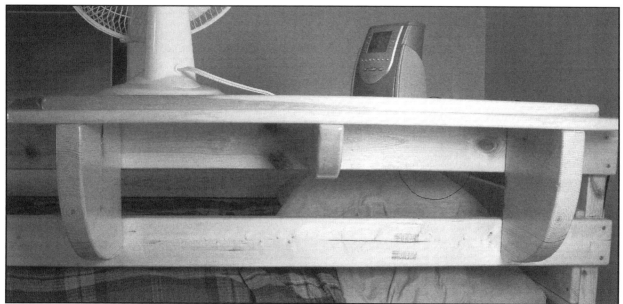

Bedside Table Installed

CHAPTER SEVEN

THE EXECUTIVE DESK OPTION

This is an awesome desk, as the available space is incredible! Anyone using multiple resources for their studies will appreciate the space this affords. The matching bookshelf should hold a year's worth of textbooks and related material. To build this, start with your shopping list.

1 – 2 x 12 x 8' SPF (38 x 286 mm x 2.4 m)
1 – ³/₄ x 23 – ¹/₄ x 96" melamine shelving
(19mm x 60 cm x 2.4 m)
1 – 2 x 2 x 8' SPF (38 x 38 mm x 2.4 m)
3 – 2 x 4 x 8' SPF (38 x 89 mm x 2.4 m)
4 – 2" deck screws (50mm)
8 – 2¹/₂" deck screws (65 mm)
8 – 3" deck screws (80 mm)
1 – 12 oz. tube construction adhesive (.35 liter)
1 – 1¹/₂" roll masking tape (4 cm)

Executive Desk

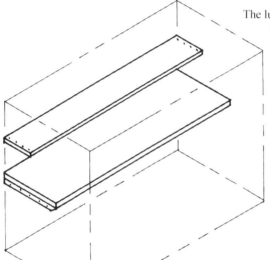

The lumber dealers where I shop carry three finishes for the melamine shelving; white, natural oak, and natural knotty pine. Naturally, I like the pine best with pine furniture. SPF is an abbreviation for spruce, pine and fir. This just means construction lumber. You could substitute a length of prefabricated countertop for the shelving material. Either one makes a nice desk surface and wears well. The main difference, besides appearance, is that countertop must be cut from the back side. This prevents the edge from chipping out real ugly. The melamine doesn't chip near as bad. Both products have one feature in common, though: their sawing debris consists of sharp, fast moving particles. Safety glasses are essential! Transport your material choices to your work area as before.

Next, move on to your cutting and shaping. This assumes you are making the standard design. If you are using the longer twin mattress; add 4" (10 cm) to these lengths. If you are reusing an existing metal spring platform, you must wait to cut all your long material to length on-site. Cut two pieces of the 2 x 2 stock to 23" long (38 x 38 mm x 58 cm). Nip off half of a corner on each of them. See drawing. Move these aside. Then cut your 2 x 12 to 79" long, (38 x 286 mm x 201 cm). (Longer if you are using the longer mattress!) Try to make a nice smooth, square cut. Touch it up with a plane and sandpaper if you need to. I make this cut using the 12" speed square (30 cm), just like chapter two. Next cut your 3 – 2 x 4s to 76" long (38 x 89 mm x 193 cm). Now, mark your wide shelving to 76" long (193 cm), just a small mark for now. Apply masking tape to one face, wrapping both edges. See photo. You need the tape about a foot wide and centering that first small mark. Now measure out that 76" length near both edges. Draw across with a straight edge, connecting your marks. Carefully support the work piece. You don't want the cut off piece dropping off and tearing out a noticeable chunk. Cut this to length with a circular saw and a new plywood blade. Touch up the cut with sand paper if necessary.

With everything cut to length, begin rounding over your wood edges. Machine the end grain first, and then

DESK LEDGER

MAKE TWO

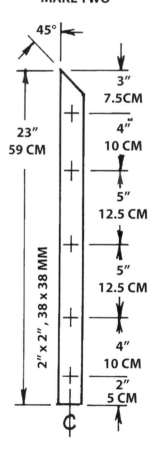

45°

3"
7.5CM

4"
10 CM

23"
59 CM

5"
12.5 CM

5"
12.5 CM

2" x 2", 38 x 38 MM

4"
10 CM

2"
5 CM

the long sides. Do not round over the melamine shelving! When you finish rounding, you can proceed to sanding. Use the 100# production paper as before. Either the belt sander or the rubber sanding block work well for this. As you sand, brush off the work piece occasionally, and feel the surface with your hand. Get all the wood uniformly smooth. Do not sand the prefinished shelving!

Next up, is applying the sealer and varnish. Dust it off and rub it well with a good tack rag before applying the sanding sealer. When this dries, turn over your wood and do the other side. Take special notice that only one side of the 2 x 4 (38 x 89 mm) stiffeners gets prefinished. The other side must remain "raw". When the sealer dries adequately, lightly sand it with the 180# paper. Dust it off, tack it off, and apply the varnish. The 2 x 12 (38 x 286 mm) will be mounted at eye level, and any runs, drips, and edge goobers will be noticed.

BOTTOM VIEW OF DESK

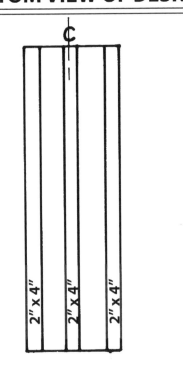

3 STIFFENERS ATTACHED

The next step is to assemble your desk surface of the prefinished shelving, and the three 2 x 4 stiffeners. You will need some large spring clamps and some construction adhesive for this. Remove any remaining tape now. Turn the shelf so that the best side is down. Wipe the surface clean with a rag dampened with mineral spirits. Apply a bead of adhesive to the unvarnished side of a 2 x 4. A wavy S-curve is the idea. Carefully turn the 2 x 4 over and apply it glue side down along one edge of you shelving. Strive to make this flush with the edge and the ends. Hold it in place with four spring clamps, equally spaced. Wait an hour and repeat with the other 2 x 4 along the other edge. Glue and clamp and wait as before. The third stiffener is attached parallel to the first two, centered in the remaining space. See drawing. Measure and mark the space. Apply your adhesive and set it in position. You will be able to clamp the two ends, but not the middle. Just set something heavy on it for the glue setting time.

Installation begins by drilling the mounting holes in the shelf and the ledgers. Each end of the 2 x 12 shelf gets four holes. See drawing. Both of the 2 x 2 ledgers get five holes. See drawing.

BOOK SHELF END
HOLE LOCATIONS

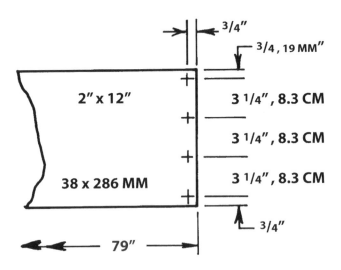

Attach the ledgers to the inside of the second rung. Flush the back ends. Flush the bottom edges, too. Fasten them with the 2½" screws (65 mm). You wouldn't want the screw points showing through, right? Now hoist the 2 x 12 shelf into place. Have someone hold it while you fasten it, or vice versa. It hangs on its screws to the bottom of the third rung. The back edge flushes with the back. You must drive a few of the 2" (50 mm) screws through the spreader into the back edge of this board. Most likely you will have to move the entire bed frame to do this. Don't skip this step. The shelf will relax down into a belly shape over time if you don't support the middle.

Lift the prefabricated desk surface into place next. It goes in easiest with one end high and one end low. Just get the low end on the ledger and slide it all the way back, and lower the other end into place. Get help for this, it isn't real heavy, but it is awkward. Next drill and screw through both of the 2 x 2 ledgers into the middle stiffener (From underneath.)

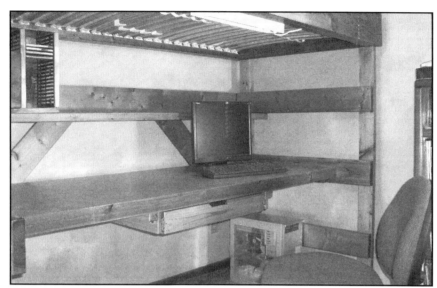

Executive Desk

Congratulations. You did it! This book shelf should hold a year's worth of textbooks, and this desk should hold your biggest projects in one place. There is also plenty of room underneath the desk to store even more stuff. Chapter 13 shows some more ideas on that subject. I also recommend some task lighting over the desk. After all, some midnight studies are par for the course, right? Chapter 9 explains some of those options, plus the cords, cables, speakers, etc., so inevitable with modern life. So read on and choose well. Set up the last of your things, give that chair a spin, and you, my friend, are in business.

CHAPTER EIGHT

THE TRANSVERSE DESK

The transverse desk is smaller than the executive desk. For many people this will be adequate. It is not for everyone. It compares in size to many dormitory supplied desks. The matching bookshelf should suffice for a semester's worth of textbooks. There is still room underneath to stack a couple of file storage tubs or the shallow pencil drawer. See photo.

Transverse Desk Installed

TRANSVERSE DESK
SECTION VIEW

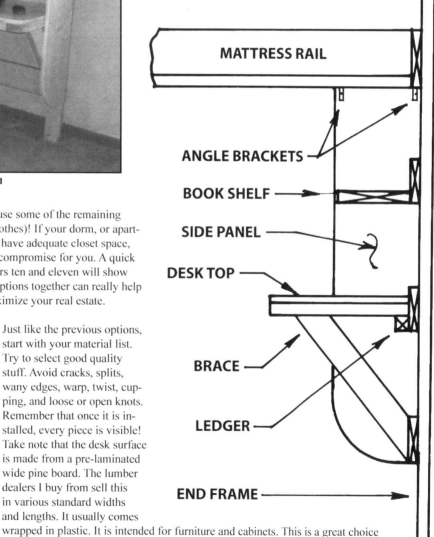

MATTRESS RAIL

ANGLE BRACKETS

BOOK SHELF

SIDE PANEL

DESK TOP

BRACE

LEDGER

END FRAME

The biggest reason to choose this option is to use some of the remaining under story area for other storage (like your clothes)! If your dorm, or apartment, or bedroom doesn't have adequate closet space, this could be a good compromise for you. A quick glance at chapters ten and eleven will show that these options together can really help to maximize your real estate.

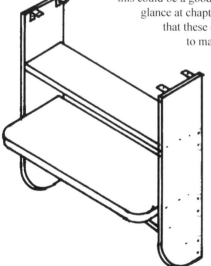

Just like the previous options, start with your material list. Try to select good quality stuff. Avoid cracks, splits, wany edges, warp, twist, cupping, and loose or open knots. Remember that once it is installed, every piece is visible! Take note that the desk surface is made from a pre-laminated wide pine board. The lumber dealers I buy from sell this in various standard widths and lengths. It usually comes wrapped in plastic. It is intended for furniture and cabinets. This is a great choice for this application. If this is not available in your area, you must make do with plywood. You will need at least an under layment grade, with all voids filled, and one side sanded to an "A" grade. You can either accept the exposed edges or apply veneer tape to them. Hopefully your lumber dealer will sell partial sheets (often called handy panels). A 2' x 4' (60 cm x 120 cm) piece will be sufficient.

2 – 1 x 12 x 4' #1 pine (19 x 286 mm x 1.25 m)
1 – 1 x 18 x 4' edge glued pine stock (19 x 460 mm x 1.25 m)
1 – 2 x 10 x 4' SPF (38 x 235 mm x 1.25 m)
2 – 2 x 4 x 8' SPF (38 x 89 mm x 1.8 m)
1 – 2 x 2 x 8' SPF (38 x 38 mm x 1.8 m)
1 – 12 oz. tube construction adhesive (.35 liter)
1# – 2" course thread screws (50 mm)
6 – 2½" course thread screws (65 mm)
4 – 3" course thread screws (80 mm)
4 – small angle brackets (3/4") (19 mm)

When you have purchased your material and brought it to your work area, you can begin the cutting and shaping. Start with your square ended pieces. Use the speed square method. Smooth out any rough cuts, and move them to the cut pile as you go.

1 – 2 x 10 x 39" lg. (38 x 235 mm x 99 cm)
1 – 2 x 2 x 39" lg. (38 x 38 mm x 99 cm)
1 – 2 x 4 x 32" lg. (38 x 89 mm x 81 cm)
2 – 2 x 4 x 18" lg. (38 x 89 mm x 46 cm)
1 – 2 x 4 x 14½" (38 x 89 mm x 36.8 cm)

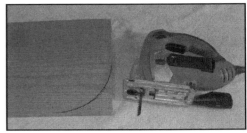
Cutting a Radius

Next, cut your side panels, as detailed in the drawing. Cut the radius as accurate as possible. Smooth out any saw marks or roughness with a spoke shave plane and sandpaper. When they are satisfactory, move them to your cut pile. Next, carefully lay out and cut the desk top from the edge glued stock, as detailed in the drawing. Plane and sand out any saw marks and mill marks. Get those tangent areas slick. Move it to the cut pile. The curved cut on the two end stiffeners can be traced from the desk top. Just make a dual reference mark for each end so they end up at the same end where they were traced. (A-A or B-B, etc..) Cut the curve as accurate as you can, and plane and smooth it too.

SIDE PANEL DETAIL

MAKE TWO

1 x 12 PINE (19 x 286 MM)

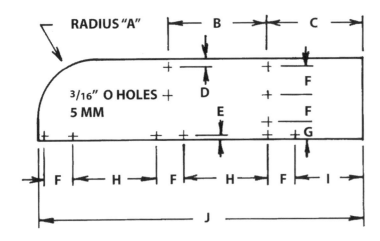

**PLANE OR SAND RADIUS SMOOTH
ROUND OVER BOTH SIDES OF AL EDGES**

A	8"	20 CM
B	14 1/2"	36.8 CM
C	13 1/2"	34.3 CM
D	1"	2.5 CM
E	3/4"	2 CM
F	4"	10.1 CM
G	2 1/4"	5.7 CM
H	12"	30.5 CM
I	9 1/2"	24.2 CM
J	46 1/4"	117.4 CM

BRACE DETAIL

MAKE TWO

40° 23 1/4" 50°
59 CM

2 x 4 SPF (38 x 89 MM)

Finally, cut the two angle braces as detailed in the drawing. The angles must be flat and true. When every piece is cut, you will again round over the edges as before.

To safely round over the 2 x 2 (38 x 38 mm) ledger, you should lay it along side a scrap 2 x 4 (38 x 89 mm). This will provide more surface area to support the router base. Every part gets the full round over treatment with the exception of the angle cuts on the angle braces. Just a light sanding for any stray wood fibers is all they need. When all the rounding over of edges is complete, you begin sanding.

DESK LEDGER

2 x 2 SPF , 38 x 38 MM

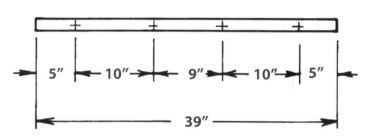

5" 10" 9" 10" 5"

39"

Make everything uniformly smooth. Remove any dirt, mill marks, grade stamps, saw marks, etc. This is your last chance to improve the appearance, so make the most of it.

DESK TOP DETAIL

SHOWN UNDERSIDE
WITH STIFFENERS APPLIED

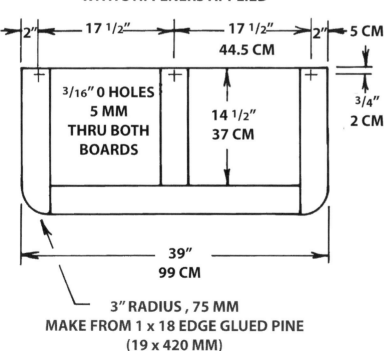

2" 17 1/2" 17 1/2" 2" 5 CM
44.5 CM

3/16" 0 HOLES
5 MM
THRU BOTH
BOARDS

14 1/2"
37 CM

3/4"
2 CM

39"
99 CM

3" RADIUS , 75 MM
MAKE FROM 1 x 18 EDGE GLUED PINE
(19 x 420 MM)

There is one sub-assembly step required before varnishing. The stiffeners must be adhered to the bottom side of the desk top. Apply an S-curving bead of construction adhesive to the laminating side of both end stiffeners. Carefully set them in position with the desk top. Lay the 32" (81 cm) stiffener loosely in between. Secure the two end stiffeners with your spring clamps. Keep the clamps on until the adhesive sets up, 20 – 60 minutes. Then attach the loose 32" board to the front edge, and attach one of the 14½" (37 cm) fillers to the rear edge. Glue and clamp these as before. Finally, attach the 11" (28 cm) stiffener (centered and across the grain) and the last 14½" filler to the rear edge. When the adhesive is cured, carefully remove any excess squeezed out. Whether gouging, or scraping or sanding, make it look good. Pay close attention to the desk top's exposed edges.

Staging is a temporary solution to facilitate a process. The pre-finishing, or varnish phase, requires more space than your saw horses currently have. They will not hold all your boards at one time. But if you attach the extra pair of 2 x 4s (38 x 89 mm) to the saw horses, you will increase the area available (a more realistic staging of the process). Drill a 3/16" (5 mm) hole 12" (30 cm) from each end of both of them. Fasten with 2½" (65 mm) screws to the saw horses. See photo. Loosely spread your components across these pieces.

Prepare the wood as before, and apply the sanding

---

sealer. Remember to use long brush strokes. Finish each board in turn before proceeding to the next one. Stopping in the middle can leave obvious lap marks. If you start brushing the farthest wood you can reach, and finish with the closest, you will walk around it less and get less on you. When the sealer is dry, turn over your wood and prepare the second side. Pay close attention to your edges. Remove any runs or drips. Sand it if necessary. Dust it off, tack it off, and apply the sealer to the second side. When that is dry, prepare as before, and apply varnish. Repeat for the second side also. The desk top should receive three coats of varnish, as it will get the most wear and abuse. Wait until all the varnish has cured out hard before installing these on your loft bed.

Now you have to layout and drill all the mounting holes in all the pieces. See detail drawings. Next, attach the two small steel angle brackets to each of the side panels, per drawing. Hoist your first side panel into place now, tight against the mattress rail at the top, and just covering the end grain of the rungs. Consult the section view drawing for proper position. The brackets should be on the inside. It is helpful to start a couple of finish nails on the frame edge between the rung and the vertical as a positioning device. Drive the 2" (50 mm) screws through the side panel into the end grain of the three rungs. Then fasten the steel angle brackets to the mattress rail, keeping the side panel square and parallel. Repeat this process for the other side panel on the other side of the loft. Carefully pull the temporary nails.

Please note how the spreader rail and diagonal brace would interfere with the side panel if mounted in their standard position. These must be attached in an alternate position, overlaying the side panel! See drawing. Carefully maintain accuracy (especially squareness) during assembly. Use the full number of screws where specified.

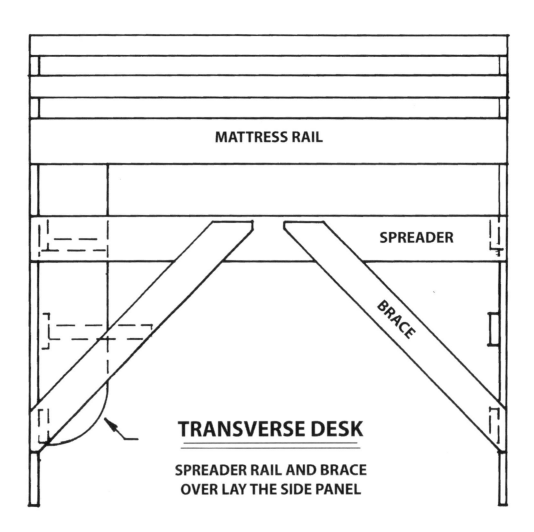

MATTRESS RAIL

SPREADER

BRACE

TRANSVERSE DESK

SPREADER RAIL AND BRACE
OVER LAY THE SIDE PANEL

The book shelf goes up next. It should fit snug between the side panels. One edge is screwed to the topmost 2 x 6 rung. (See drawing for hole location.) Sink all of the 3" (80 mm) screws here. See drawing. Next, pull the outer edge into alignment with your upper square mark

SHELF SUPPORT

HOLE LOCATION DETAIL
CENTERED

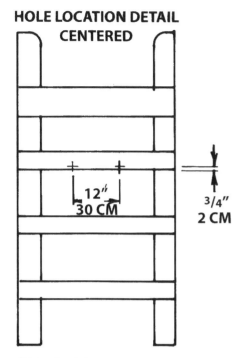

12"
30 CM

3/4"
2 CM

STANDARD END FRAME

on the side panel, and fasten with 2" (50 mm) screws. Do this for both ends and side panels. The 2 x 2 desk ledger is next. Hold it flush to the bottom edge of the second 2 x 6 rung. Fasten with the 2½" (65 mm) screws. You may need to start a couple more temporary nails to help hold the desk top. Drive two eight penny (60 mm) finish nails into the bottom square mark of both side panels.

Slip the desk top into place next. The back edge should rest securely on the ledger and the front edge on those two nails. Hold it tight against the rung and all the way down to the ledger, and fasten it with more 3" (80 mm) screws along the back edge. Next drive the screws through the side panel into the stiffener. Fasten both side panels into both ends of the desk top.

Finally, attach the two wooden angle braces, to permanently support the desk top. Hold one in place, make a couple pencil marks, and pre-drill the side panel. Hold the brace up again, and fasten it with more 2" (50 mm) screws. Now you can drive the 3" (80 mm) screws through the angle cuts into the stiffener and rung. Repeat this for the second brace and you are done. Your desk should feel pretty solid now. Just add some task lighting and you are good to go!

Transverse Desk Installed

CHAPTER NINE

CABLE UP!

The user of a loft bed with a desk/study area will need electrical power and wiring for all their small appliances. These can really add up. The bedside table might typically hold a clock-radio, an oscillating fan, cell phone charger, and maybe a night light. The desk/study area could also have task lighting, laptop charger, scanner, printer, desk top components, game system, television, CD player/MP3/iPod dock, digital camera dock, etc. A mini-fridge and a microwave in the room could prove real handy too. You may have some, all, or more of these.

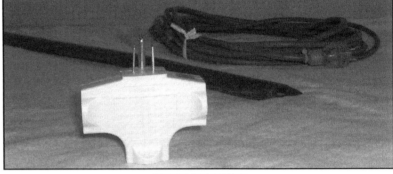
Extension Cord and More

There is also the low voltage and data transmission cabling between components to allow for. Always try to rout these separately from your power cords. If they are too close, weird stuff can happen to your data. In the same way that sound speakers are susceptible to distortion, hum, and feedback; the data cabling is also. The effect on your computer could look like voodoo! Some TVs, and microwaves leak stray radiation that affects your computer monitor. Try to avoid using the older ones, or at least keep them on the other side of the room.

Use the best quality cables and wires available for data transmission. The grade of insulation, the wire itself, and especially the connectors, can make a noticeable difference. Better stuff just works better. This isn't the place to shave off $10. Hopefully, your campus or neighborhood has a wireless internet system with only an antenna device needed to access. But if you have a cable system, DSL, or dial-up, be sure to use the best quality cables to your modem. Sometimes the gold standard of connections is actually gold! Your local consumer electronics retailer should have the most current information and materials for this.

Task lighting at your desk is also essential. Put the light where you need it! I feel that the under mounted fixture is better for this than a free standing lamp as it helps define the study area and is less likely to fall and break. There are also some lamps made to clamp on to the edge of a desk, shelf, or table. This could be a good compromise between the bulky free standing lamp and the under mounted fixture (out of the way). Whichever you choose, try to set it up so that no shadow is cast on your work or study material.

The lighting types I have found are; incandescent, fluorescent, halogen and xenon. Incandescent is the least favored because it consumes a lot of wattage, and it produces the most heat. This is followed by halogen, and xenon, and fluorescent. The type of light produced can make or break your desk experience. There are a great variety of fixtures available. These run through a gamut of light intensity, color, contrast, and wattage. You must sort through it to determine what will meet your needs; and just what are those needs?

You need sufficient light to read text easily, day or night. After all, some midnight studies are par for the course, right? A good rule of thumb I've heard is, you need 600 to 800 LUX (lumens/square meter) at your work surface, minimum. Most lamps (bulbs, elements, tubes) have a light measurement, in "lumens", on their package. So, just buy something with enough lumens.

The color of light matters too: cool white, soft white, warm white, and full spectrum. This is personal preference to some degree, but the wrong choice can give you eye strain, headaches, and make reading unpleasant. I personally like full spectrum light, as it approximates natural sun light. The contrast is good, too.

I have a free standing task light in my office. It has a large, heavy base, and is very stable. It produces full spectrum light, of a color and brightness and contrast that is very easy on the eyes. It has a specialized fluorescent lamp that only consumes 27 watts of electricity, and produces very little heat. This is a good choice if you have room for it. I do. My desk is huge.

My son's loft bed with desk, has an 18" (46 cm) fluorescent fixture, with full spectrum light. This consumes 15 watts of electricity. I can not feel any heat from it. It produces 600 lumens, according to the label. We have it mounted to the under side of the bed slats. This seems ideal! The 18" tubes, available in my area produce a light range of 400–1000 lumens, depending on the color spectrum chosen.

I had hoped that the 12" (30 cm) size would suffice, but they seemed to top out at 400 lumens of light produced. I guess that explains why reading by them is so tiring. The 12" size isn't adequate, nor are many of the gimmick lights sold today. If you stick with the rule of thumb, you will be fine.

Your sound speakers can be moved around a large desk, book shelf, entire under story area, or even the entire room to optimize the sound quality. Besides just sitting loose, they can be attached at any height, with brackets or clamps. Again, see your consumer electronics retailer.

For some people, music enhances their study and learning. For others, it distracts or even prevents it. This probably applies to all forms of entertainment. You have to evaluate your own learning style and priorities, and discipline yourself accordingly. If you share a room with one or more people, you will have to negotiate! Besides roommates, there may be building rules to consider. Respecting other's needs can go a long ways to legitimizing your own. Headphones can be a discreet solution at times…

The existing electrical receptacles, and their capacity, will determine your power cords and distribution. If the building is new, or recently upgraded, you no doubt have lots of plugs, and plenty of capacity. If it is thirty years old, there are probably a lot fewer plugs, but still plenty of capacity. If the building is forty years old, or more; the electrical cabling could be challenging. You might find two prong ungrounded receptacles versus the three prong grounded type. There might be fuses instead of breakers. And, quite likely, it is under capacity. This would manifest as frequently tripped breakers or blown fuses. With a little use and awareness, you will probably figure out which receptacles are on which circuits. Hopefully, that doesn't work out to rigid scheduling of your large wattage appliances; (hair dryers and toasters from 7am to 8am [0700 to 0800] only?) . Most people would prefer to run more extension cords to tap other circuits.

Semipermanent extension cords should be semipermanently attached. Keep them neat and safe. Avoid crossing walkways, if at all possible! If your cord must cross a walkway, use a tapered cable tunnel and secure it. These are available where office supplies are sold. Properly used, these prevent tripping hazards and dangerous wear to the cords themselves.

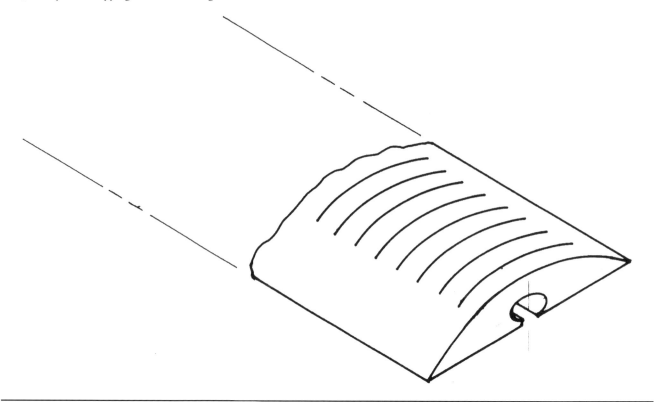

If your room or apartment has two prong receptacles; get some adaptor plugs, and attach them with the center screw. Never cut off the grounding prong from your cords. The adaptors are cheap!

Surge Protector and More

Use good quality extension cords, at least 16 gauge, if supplying two or more small usage devices, or one larger one. If the cord gets hot, it is too skinny! If it has worn or broken areas, replace it. Ten dollars spent could prevent a nasty shock, or even a fire. That's a no-brainer!

A couple of hard rubber splitter plugs could simplify your power supply cabling, but don't over load them. Remember, the receptacle still only has its rated wattage.

You are going to need surge protectors for all your vulnerable appliances, like computers and televisions. These go between the extension cord or receptacle, and your device. They come in many different sizes, shapes, types, and ratings. I am told that a 1000 joules rating of protection is required. Most types cannot be "reset". They last for one large surge, or several smaller ones. After that, they don't protect. It is a good idea to replace them every year, since you cannot "read" or test most types.

A lot of people believe that a power strip is a surge protector. This is not necessarily true! Unless it is labeled as a surge protector, it is not! Most power strips do have over current protection however. This is usually in the form of a breaker switch with an indicator light. Over current protection is a really good idea. If you can find a surge protector of adequate capacity, multiple outlets, and over current protection, that is ideal!

Many large buildings such as schools and offices, have in-line equipment, that perform the same functions as your surge protector. Unless you know for sure, use one anyway.

Never run your power tools, or large home appliances, through your computer's surge protector. Those devices don't need the same delicate range of exact current, and they can really chew things up with their own surges and fluctuations of power and current.

Try to make a neat job of the cabling, branch off for each device, bundle and secure them with the appropriate hardware. Remember; loose cords aren't just ugly, they are accident prone!

Some helpful wiring hardware are: cable grommets, zip ties, strap clamps, shielded staples, and tape. Grommets protect cables and cords from sharp edges, where they pass through hard surfaces, like desks, cabinets, and junction boxes.

Zip ties have a ratchet head and a toothed rack or stem. When fastened around a cable bundle and adjacent structure, they make an easy way to safely tie off. They are also easily removed with a wire cutter. Zip ties are available in a variety of colors and sizes. Variety packs with two or three sizes are commonly sold. You will need some four inch, eight inch, and some eleven inch ties. I prefer the appearance of the white color against the light colored wood. Black draws attention to itself, as do colors like pink and chartreuse. But as always, the user must decide!

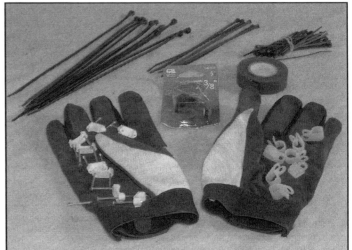
Wiring Supplies

Strap clamps are plastic straps that wrap a cord loosely, and secure to the structure with a screw. Sometimes, these come with a peel and stick back. Shielded staples pound in with a hammer. (Do you really want to make those holes)?

This chapter is certainly not a definitive wiring guide for an electrician, or a cable guy. I hope this includes enough tips and practical sense to be helpful. The goal is: You safely using your stuff. The photos show real examples, but your room may be laid out very different, with more or less capacity. If you are uncertain about anything, get qualified advice!. Remember, asking questions is always ok! Get the best information you can. Informed choices are usually the good ones. Good luck to you.

CHAPTER TEN

SHELF STORAGE SYSTEM

T his is a 16" (40 cm) deep shelf cabinet. It is sized to fit under the mattress rail. It is oriented parallel to the end frame. This cabinet has two permanent shelves and three large spaces. It has an open front and a plywood back. It should be attached to the bed frame.

The open shelf cabinet can hold folded stacks of clothing, linens, sporting goods, etc. This system can be fitted with simple drawers, to function like a bureau. It can also hold a wide range of containers. These would include; storage tubs, boxes, crates, and baskets. The main idea here is large and rectangular. (A pair of legal size file boxes per shelf is awesome!)

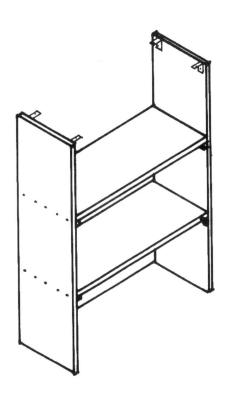

Shelf System with Drawers, etc.

The exposed side panel can support several robe hooks for jackets, clothing, backpacks, gym bag, etc.

The material of choice for the sides and shelves is 1 x 16 (19 mm x 40 cm) edge-glued pine. This material comes in various widths and lengths. It is usually sanded smooth and wrapped in plastic. It is intended for furniture making and cabinets. If this not available in your area, you must make do with plywood. At least get an A-B grade, with the voids filled and the surface sanded. (Veneer tape applied to the exposed end grain helps the appearance of plywood.)

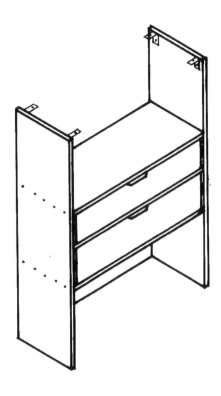

This chapter will show how to build three different configurations of the open shelf cabinet. The following chapter explains how to build the drawers and some simple containers. There are also many containers sold by discount retailers that work well with this system. So make your choices, copy the appropriate material lists, and let's go shopping!

Option I material list

2–1 x 16 x 72" edge glued pine boards (19 mm x 40 cm x 1.8 m)
2–1 x 16 x 48" edge glued pine boards (19 mm x 40 cm x 1.25 m)
$^1/_2$ x $^3/_4$ x 72" pine blind stop (12 x 18 mm x 1.8 m)
1–1 x 3 x 48" #2 pine (19 x 70 mm x 1.25 m)
1– $^1/_4$" x 4 x 8 pine or luan plywood (light colored) (7 mm x 1.25 m x 2.4 m)
4– 1$^1/_2$" steel angle brackets with short screws (40 mm)
1– small bottle of wood glue
20 – 1" brads (25 mm)
40 – 3d galvanized box nails (30 mm)
20 – 8d finish nails (60 mm)

Option II material list addition:

1 – 1 x 3 x 48" #2 pine (19 x 70 mm x 1.25 m)
2 – drawers with hardware from the following chapter.

Option III material list

1 – 1 x 16 x 72" edge glued pine boards (19 mm x 40 cm x 1.8 m)
1 – 1 x 16 x 48" edge glued pine boards (19 mm x 40 cm x 1.25 cm)
$^1/_2$ x $^3/_4$ x 36" pine blind stop (12 x 18 mm x 1 m)
5 – 1 x 3 x 48" #2 pine (19 x 70 mm x 1.25 m)
1 – $^1/_4$" x 4 x 8 pine or luan plywood (light colored) (7 mm x 1.25 x 2.4 m)
4 – drawers with hardware from the following chapter
4 – 1$^1/_2$" steel angle brackets with short screws (40 mm)
1 – small bottle of wood glue
10 – 1" brads (25 mm)
40 – 3d galvanized box nails (30 mm)
50 – 8d finish nails (60 mm)

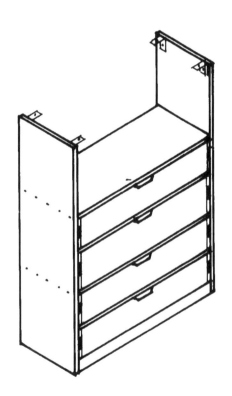

When you get your material back to your work area, set it up on your sawhorses. Make sure the edge glued stock is all 16" wide! (40 cm) Unwrap the plastic from the wood. Mark and cut the two longer boards to 56½" (143.5 cm) long. Then cut the two shorter boards to 37½" (95.2 cm) long, and the 1 x 3 to 37½" long. Next, cut the blind stop into four pieces of 16" (40 cm) long each. Finally, cut the plywood to 39" x 38½". (99 x 98 cm). (The other half sheet can serve as drawer bottoms or other container parts.)

Slightly round all the edges with some 100# sandpaper. Try to remove anything sharp or rough, especially dress the cut ends of the blind stop.

Next, you must lay out the shelf locations on the side panels. I like to lay them together on the sawhorses for this, back to back. Measure up from the bottom, near both edges of both panels, and square across. Make a small "x" on the bottom side of the each line. These are for the shelf cleats (your blind stop). The shelf cleats must be thinner than the drawer glides. (Most are actually ⁷⁄₁₆" thick.) If they are not thinner, the drawers will rub on them! (Base shoe molding is an excellent substitute)!

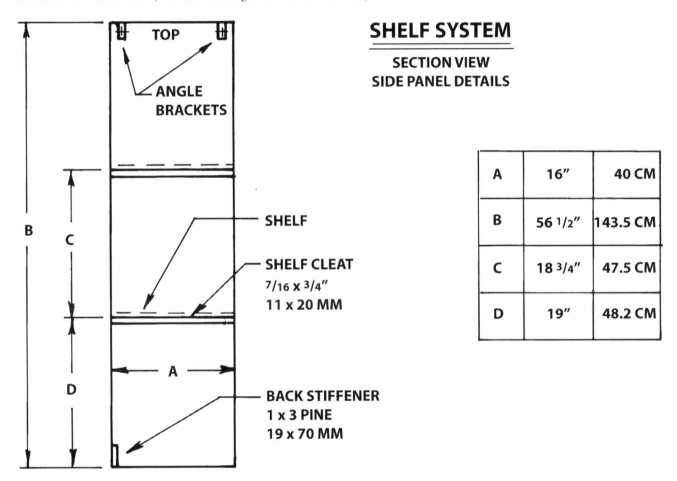

SHELF SYSTEM

SECTION VIEW
SIDE PANEL DETAILS

A	16"	40 CM
B	56 1/2"	143.5 CM
C	18 3/4"	47.5 CM
D	19"	48.2 CM

Working one at a time, run a fine bead of wood glue to the "x" side, all the way across, and apply a piece of blind stop there. Secure both ends with spring clamps, keeping exactly on the line. Permanently secure with four equally spaced brads. Do all four shelf cleats likewise. If any wood glue squeezes out, you can wipe it off with a damp cloth, while still wet.

Once all the glue is dry, you can touch up any sanding that is necessary. Dust them off, tack them off, and apply sanding sealer to the surface and edges. When the sealer is dry, flip your boards over and prepare that side. As always; scrape off any runs, drips or goobers, touching up any sanding as needed. Dust them off, tack them off, and apply sanding sealer to the second side. Wipe the edges with a cloth to coat them thinly. When this sealer is dry; lightly sand it with fine grit paper. Dust it off, tack it off and apply spar-varnish. Thinly coat the edges with a cloth as before. Repeat for your last side. Let everything cure out hard before assembling.

Drill some starter holes for the shelves. These should be ³⁄₃₂" (3 mm) diameter. Make those holes as perpendicular to the board as you can. Repeat for all four shelf locations. See photo.

Move the side panels and shelves to the floor for assembly. Apply a thin bead of construction adhesive to the bearing surface of your first cleat. Tip the side panel up on edge and bring the first shelf into position. See photo. Hold the shelf tight against the cleat and drive the first finish nail near the top edge. Drive the bottom nail likewise, and the two intermediate, after that. Fastening the opposite edges first helps keep it on the marks. Repeat this for the second shelf. When that is secure, begin the second side panel. Just glue and nail one shelf at a time. It should still warp and wrack easily enough to apply the glue on the last cleat. Take care to make all the front edges flush.

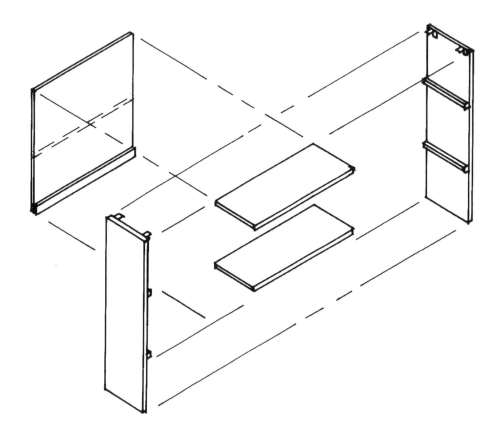

Decide side which is the back now. Apply some glue to both ends of the 1 x 3 (19 x 70 mm) stiffener, and insert it in place. Fasten it with two 8d (60 mm) finish nails per end. It is easier to pre-drill through the sides before nailing the parting rail. Use a ³/₃₂" (3 mm) drill bit. If you stagger them a little, you are less likely to split the wood along the grain line. Lastly, put the plywood back in place. This will permanently hold the structure to its desired form, so adjust the shape as you nail it off. Align the top edge to the top of the top shelf and the side edge to the side panel. Nail off the side edge first. Start 2" from the top corner (5 cm) and then 4" on center from there (10 cm). Use the three penny box nails (30 mm) for this. Pound them in straight! When the side is done, proceed to the top edge. Adjust the far top corner to match the plywood shape. Nail that corner first. Finish off the top edge, then the second side, and finally the bottom. Since the bottom edge is nailed into the stiffener, you must cut those nails short. (If not, you would see them sticking through the other side)! Make them about ¾" long (19 mm). A wire cutter works well for this.

That's it! The open shelf is built. Just stand it up, and carefully maneuver it into position, under your loft. This is easier if someone lifts the loft bed for you while you maneuver. Hold the cabinet back about 3" (8 cm) from the rungs. (That should keep your feet out of it when you climb.) Fasten the two sides to the mattress rails with some angle brackets, on the inside. You are done, you are good to go!

Open shelf option II adds to what you have already built, see photo. Two drawers must be installed in the center space, and a parting rail also. It would be easiest to add these before assembling the shelf cabinet, although it can certainly be done later.

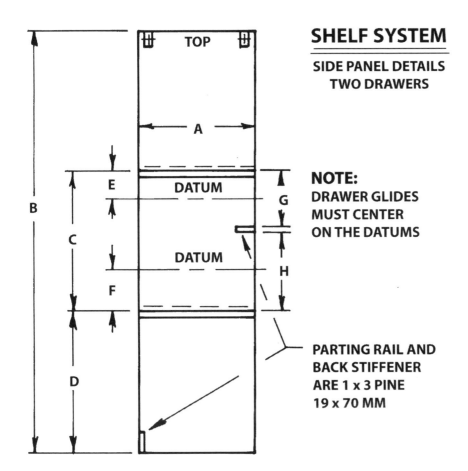

SHELF SYSTEM

SIDE PANEL DETAILS
TWO DRAWERS

NOTE:
DRAWER GLIDES
MUST CENTER
ON THE DATUMS

PARTING RAIL AND
BACK STIFFENER
ARE 1 x 3 PINE
19 x 70 MM

A	16″	40 CM
B	56 1/2″	143.5 CM
C	18 3/4″	47.5 CM
D	19″	48.2 CM
E	3 13/16″	9.6 CM
F	5 9/16″	14.2 CM
G	7 5/8″	19.4 CM
H	10 3/8″	26.3 CM

Cut the parting rail (1 x 3 pine board) to 37½″ long (19 x 70 mm x 95.2 cm). Sand it smooth and pre-finish it to match everything else.

Carefully layout the two datum lines for each side panel, as per detail drawing. Then mark the parting rail location.

Next you will attach the drawer glide hardware. They usually break down into two pieces; an inner piece and an outer piece. The inner piece attaches to the drawer sides. The outer piece attaches to the side panel. The center line of holes will correspond to the datum line you drew. Hold the end flush to the front edge of the panel, and fasten it with the screws included. Install all four glides likewise. Keep those holes centered on the datum. The shelves and the plywood back assemble the same as option I, whichever order you are building it in. Drill the starting holes for the parting rail location, on each side. Apply a little glue to each end of the 1 x 3 parting rail and put it in place. Hold it on its marks and nail it carefully with two 8d (30 mm) finish nails at each end.

The center space is ready for drawers (Described in the next chapter.) Insert the bottom, larger drawer first. The drawer glides halves need some guidance to connect. Once they start, push the whole drawer straight in. When you hear the "keeper" click, it is seated. This will prevent the drawer from falling out when extended. Repeat this procedure for the second drawer. Now to use those other spaces…

Option III, adds two more drawers to the package. This still leaves the top shelf wide open. You can keep more containers there or display keepsakes. If you are planning this from the beginning, you can save yourself one shelf board. See detail drawing. It has three parting rails and a front skirt board (plus the drawers) instead.

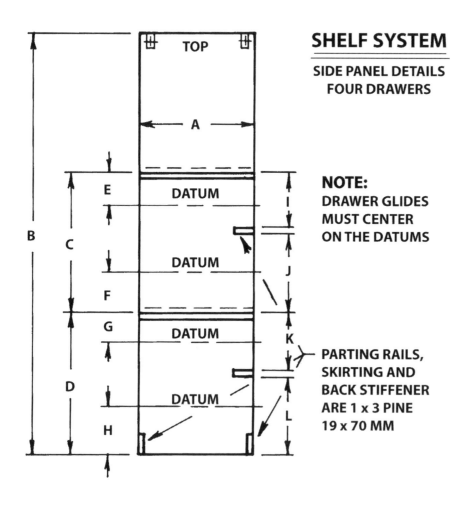

SHELF SYSTEM

SIDE PANEL DETAILS
FOUR DRAWERS

NOTE:
DRAWER GLIDES
MUST CENTER
ON THE DATUMS

PARTING RAILS,
SKIRTING AND
BACK STIFFENER
ARE 1 x 3 PINE
19 x 70 MM

A	16″	40 CM
B	56 1/2″	143.5 CM
C	18 3/4″	47.5 CM
D	19″	48.2 CM
E	3 13/16″	9.6 CM
F	5 9/16″	14.2 CM
G	3 7/8″	9.8 CM
H	6 5/8″	16.8 CM
I	7 5/8″	19.3 CM
J	10 3/8″	26.3 CM
K	7 3/4″	19.7 CM
L	10 1/2″	26.6 CM

Cut the additional 1 x 3s to length (19 x 70 mm) sand smooth, and varnish to match. Lay out the additional datums (or reference line) and parting rail locations, per drawing. Attach all drawer glide outer halves to their datums, prior to assembly of the cabinet. You can retrofit, of course, but working on it flat and open is easier!

When you assemble the unit; install the top shelf first, followed by the back stiffener. Next, install the plywood back, then the front skirt board. Finish off with the parting rails. These must be nailed exactly on their marks! Pre-drill the starting holes to make it easier. Align the front edges, and keep them flat. A pair of clamps and some scrap wood can help you achieve the desired quality. See photo. Don't forget to set the nails when you are finished.

When all the rails are secured, the cabinet is built. You can stand it up and insert the drawers. Transport it to your new living space as any furniture. Moving and installing this will require at least two people. This is not all that heavy, but it is bulky. The bed frame, however, is heavy. Once you have this on-site, carefully slide it into place under the mattress rails. If it is going on the same end that you climb; you should fasten it about 3" (8 cm) back from the rungs. Use those 1½" (40 mm) steel angle brackets, on the insides. Only short screws please!

Shelf System with Drawers, etc.

I recommend the addition of a few clothes hooks to the exposed side panel. (Do this on-site.) Now you are ready for business.

CHAPTER ELEVEN

DRAWERS AND MORE

The intent of this chapter is to demonstrate the building of some drawers, containers and useful storage. These will work with the open shelf system in chapter ten or the desk with bookshelf in chapters seven and eight. The woodworking technology has been simplified so that a novice who is handy can build these. The million dollar workshop with large stationary power tools won't be needed. The same few handheld tools, used throughout this book, will suffice. I will begin with drawers. Chapter ten, option II, has two drawers, and option III, has four drawers. The desks can also be fitted with a shallow drawer. Drawers combined with crates, tubs, boxes, or baskets, work well, too. This is a storage system that can work for you.

Simple drawers are large sturdy drawers with all the construction details simplified. These drawers are very handy to use and quite attractive. They can be made a variety of height dimensions (volume) just by using wider or narrower boards. Nominal width lumber is used where ever possible. A single notch handle and good quality extension glides complete the package.

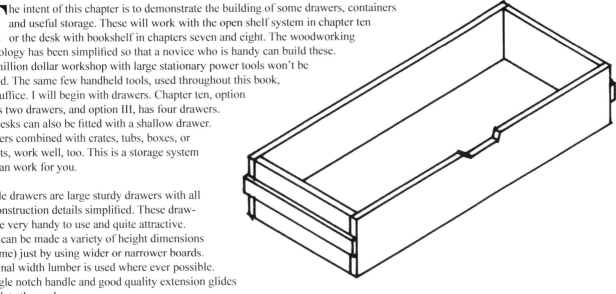

The sample configuration is for the middle space. Since that space is 18" high (46 cm), we will make two drawers; of 1 x 8 lumber, and 1 x 10 lumber (19 x 184 mm and 19 x 235 mm). This leaves some small clearance gaps between drawers and shelves. These drawers are of a useful and versatile size. The bottom cabinet space can also be fitted with drawers (option III). I don't recommend drawers for the top space, though. How would you see what's in them anyway? The moveable containers are great for the top space. Perhaps some display area is desired for photos, keepsakes, etc. Make your selections, copy the appropriate material lists, and let's go shopping!

1 – 1 x 8 x 10', #2 pine (19 x 184 mm x 3 m)
1 – ¼" plywood handy panel, sanded smooth (7 mm x 60 cm x 120 cm)
1 – ½ x ¾ x 9' pine blind stop (12 x 18 mm x 3 m)
12 – 8d finish nails (60 mm)
25 – 1" brads (25 mm)
1 – small bottle wood glue
1 – 12 oz. tube construction adhesive (.35 liter)
2 – 16" side mount, full extension, drawer glides (40 cm)

SECOND DRAWER

1 – 1 x 10 x 10', #2pine (19 x 235 mm x 3 m)
1 – ¼" plywood handy panel, sanded smooth(7 mm x 50 cm x 120 cm)
1 – ½ x ¾ x 9' pine blind stop (12 x 18 mm x 3 m)
16 – 8d finish nails (60 mm)
25 – 1" brads (25 mm)
1 – small bottle wood glue
1 – 12 0z. tube construction adhesive (.35 liter)
2 – 16" side mount, full extension, drawer glides (40 cm)

Note that you can cut the 10'(3 m) boards in half for transport (2–5') and the 9' of blind stop, too. If you are making the over size crates, you will have enough large scrap from the ¼" (7 mm) plywood for your drawer bottom panels. No need to buy those twice. The same small bottle of wood glue should suffice for both drawers, and the construction adhesive too.

Once you get your material back to your work area, sort it by project, not size. Cut all four sides, and bottom, for each drawer, before starting another. You will notice the four sides are basically just two lengths to cut. See drawing. Make one long side and one short side from each of the 5' boards (152 cm). Carefully, make those ends square. Assembly goes easier and looks better too.

You need a front and a back piece; each 36½" long (92.7 cm). You also need two short sides 14½" long (37 cm) and a bottom panel of ¼" plywood; 14½" x 35" (7 mm x 37 cm x 88.9 cm). Cut the blind stop to 13½", and 35" (86.3cm), two of each. The blind stops are the bottom support. These will be glued and nailed to the inside bottom edge of all four sides. Attach the long stop pieces to the long sides first with wood glue. Clamp the ends while you add the brads to secure it, equally spaced.

Next draw in place the handle notch, and carefully cut it out. Sand the notch smooth. Remember, your hand goes in the handle! Mark and drill both ends of your front and back sides. Now you are ready to assemble.

Pre-Drilling a Board End

Apply a thin bead of wood glue to the end grain of one of the short sides. Now hold your front board up on edge, and position the same short side, at 90 degrees to it, forming a corner. (This should sandwich the glue.) Temporarily secure with masking tape. Make sure the bottom cleat is oriented properly and the corner fits flush. When ready, drive an eight penny finish nail in the top starter hole. (It helps if the back end of the short side is butted against a wall for this.) Re-check the corner alignment, and drive the bottom nail. Repeat this for the other end and the other short side. Now spin the assembly 180 degrees, and attach the back side. Then turn it up on edge and drive the missing nails, both front and back. Go ahead and set the nails properly.

Next you apply a thin bead of wood glue along the bottom inner edge of a short side. Fit a piece of blind stop there, see drawing. Hold it temporarily with clamps and secure with more 1" brads (25 mm). Work your way along, keeping the bottom edges flush. Keep the brads about 8"–10" (20–25 cm) apart. Repeat for the last side. Stand it right side up when all the bottom support cleats are

Drawer Assembly

TYPICAL DRAWER SECTION

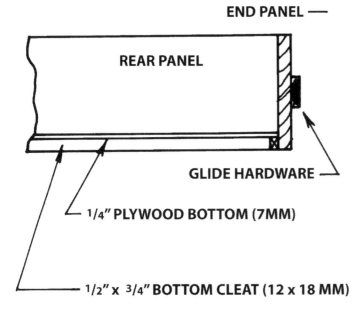

END PANEL ——

REAR PANEL

GLIDE HARDWARE ——

1/4" PLYWOOD BOTTOM (7MM)

1/2" x 3/4" BOTTOM CLEAT (12 x 18 MM)

ready. Trial fit the bottom panel now. Hold it on edge, the long way, and then the short way. Sand it smaller if you need to. I cut them with a plywood blade,(very fine). I also hold the skinny saw kerf on the wrong side of the line on purpose. This makes the panel about 1/16" (2 mm) undersize in both directions. When you are sure the panel fits, apply an ⅛" (4 mm) bead of construction adhesive on the top edge of the cleats (blind stops) all the way around. Set your plywood panel down into it with the best side up. Hold it in place with something heavy, until the glue cures. You may have to wrack the drawer shape into square in the process. The panel will hold it there permanently.

Attaching Bottom Cleats

Securing Drawer Bottom

While you are waiting for the adhesive to cure; build the second drawer. While you wait for that to cure, sand out the first drawer with 100# sandpaper. Make everything smooth, and slightly round over all the edges. When your eye and your hand agree that it is good enough, you are ready for varnish. Sand the second drawer smooth likewise.

Brush off the dust and tack it off. Try to apply the sealer thinly, as it runs badly from vertical surfaces. When it is dry, lightly sand it with your fine paper. Dust it off and wipe it with your tack rag, before applying the spar varnish. I actually vacuum the inside of drawers before varnishing. Just a little bit of fine dust will look like grit in your new finish. Allow the varnish to cure out hard before moving.

To attach the drawer glides; you have to disassemble them. Most have a small lever or spring catch to release. See photo. The inner, skinny half, goes on the drawer side. The outer, wider half, attaches to the cabinet carcass. Measure halfway up the height of your drawer ends. The 1 x 8 drawers (19 x 235 mm) get a datum line at 3⅝" (9.2 cm) from the bottom edge. Draw it front to back on both ends. The 1 x 10 drawers (19 x 235 mm) get their datum line at 4⅝" (11.7 cm) from the bottom edge. Hold the drawer glide half on the drawer side centering the holes on the datum line and the end flush with drawer front. Mark the holes with a sharp pencil. Repeat for the other end. Drill pilot holes for all, and don't go through! Attach the glide hardware with the screws provided. A pilot hole is the root diameter of a wood screw. You can judge the size by visual comparison.

Next, measure and mark the datum lines in the cabinet middle space. Measure down from the upper shelf 4⅛" (10.5 cm), front and back, for both panels. Then measure 5⅛" (13 cm) up from the bottom. Mark it front and back for both sides. Carefully draw these all the way across. Next, hold up an outer half of a drawer glide. Center the holes on the datum line, and flush the end with the cabinet front. Mark the holes with a sharp pencil. Drill pilot holes for all. You can easily measure the depth

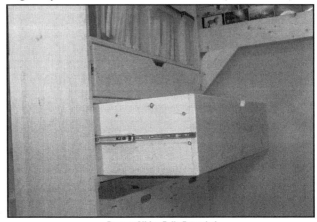

Drawer Glides Fully Extended

of drilled holes by wrapping some masking tape around your drill bit, at the desired depth measurement. When the tape reaches the wood surface, it is deep enough. Attach all the glide hard ware with the screws provided.

Put the drawers in next, and you have got it. Guide the drawer glide halves together, individually, to connect. Then push the drawer all the way in until you hear the "keeper" device click, on both sides. That means they are ready to use. They will fully extend without tipping or spilling. It is pretty cool.

THE SHALLOW DRAWER

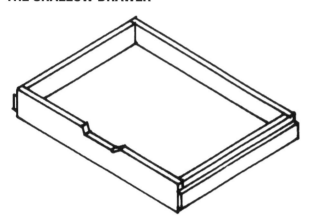

Shallow Drawer in Use

The shallow drawer is intended to be under mounted to a desk. This works well with the large executive size desk in chapter seven, or the transverse desk in chapter eight. The construction details are identical, both are intended to be centered. The same style drawer glides are used as well. The shallow drawer can store all your usual desk supplies.

Material list

    1 – 1 x 4 x 10', #2 pine (19 x 89 mm x 3 m)
    1 – ¹/₂ x ³/₄ x 8' blind stop (12 x 18 mm x 2.4 m)
    1 – ¹/₄" plywood scrap; 16 x 24 (7 mm x 40 cm x 60 cm)
    1 – 2 x 2 x 4' SPF (38 x 38 mm x 1.25 m)
    2 – 16" full extension drawer glides, side mounted (40 cm)
    8 – 8d finish nails (60 cm)
    24 – 1" brads (25 mm)
    4 – 2¹/₂" screws (65 mm)
    6 – 2" screws (50 mm)
    1 – small bottle wood glue
    1 – 12 0z. tube construction adhesive (.35 liter)

Begin by cutting two pieces of the 1 x 4 stock (19 x 89 mm) to 24" (61 cm), then two pieces to 16" (40.5 cm), and then two pieces to 14¹/₂" (37 cm). Cut your blind stop to use as bottom support cleats as follows; two pieces at 13¹/₂", and two pieces at 22¹/₂" (57 cm). Then cut your bottom panel to 14¹/₂" x 22¹/₂" (37 cm x 57 cm). (I actually cut them about ¹/₁₆" shy [2 mm], in both directions on purpose. That way it easily fits without forcing it.) Select which is the front side board, and draw the notch handle. Cut out the notch with your coping saw, like the other drawer. Sand the notch nice and smooth. Pre-drill your nail starter holes on both ends of the front side board and the back side board.

Fasten the long pieces of blind stop to the long sides with wood glue, clamps, and brads. (Just like the other drawer.) Assemble the drawer sides just like the previous one, with the 8d finish nails (60 mm). Attach the last two blind stop to the last two sides. Add the bottom panel, and secure with construction adhesive. Temporarily hold with something heavy.

While you wait for the glue to dry, prefabricate the two mounting rails. These are made of 16" (40 cm) long pieces of wood. Pre-drill the screw starter holes through the 1 x 4s (19 x 89 mm). Apply a bead of wood glue there, and sandwich with the 2 x 2 (38 x 38 mm). Keep the ends flush, and secure with 2" screws. Make two of these identical.

When all the glue is dry, scrape or sand off any excess, or squeeze out. Sand all the wood smooth, and varnish to match.

Next you must measure and lay out all four of the datums. Both of the short sides of the drawer receive a centered front to back line or 1 3/4" (45 mm). The mounting rails have it about 1/4" (7 mm) lower for clearance. This is a total of 2" down from the top edge (52 mm). Go ahead and attach the drawer glides to the drawer sides and mounting rails, just like the other drawer. Now you can measure and mark the mounting holes in the 2 x 2 (38 x 38 mm) mounting flange, per drawing. Drill them all with a 3/16" bit (5 mm).

THE SHALLOW DRAWER

UNDERMOUNTED

FRONT VIEW

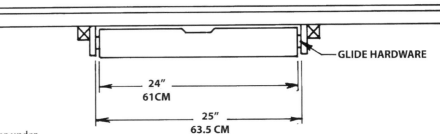

GLIDE HARDWARE

24"
61CM

25"
63.5 CM

The standard mounting rails are intended for under mounting in the center of the desk span. Installation begins by measuring the center of the desk length. Square this mark across the front and center stiffeners (bottom side). Measure out 12 1/2" (31.8 cm) in both directions, on both stiffeners, to make a 25" space (63.5 cm). Draw these in dark. Hold up your first mounting rail in position, and secure with the 2 1/2" screws (65 mm) into the stiffeners. Repeat this for the second rail. Note the configuration in the drawing. It is a good idea to hold them back from the desk's front edge 1 1/2" (4 cm). Insert the drawer into the space described by the mounting rails, and connect the drawer glide halves. Push it back until the "keeper" device clicks.

MOUNTING RAIL

MAKE TWO

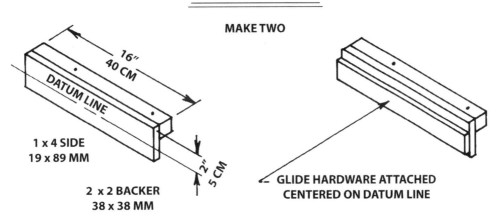

16"
40 CM

DATUM LINE

1 x 4 SIDE
19 x 89 MM

2"
5 CM

2 x 2 BACKER
38 x 38 MM

GLIDE HARDWARE ATTACHED
CENTERED ON DATUM LINE

To install the shallow drawer under the transverse desk; you should attach the mounting rails to the bottom of the desk stiffeners. Lay out the 25" wide space centered in the 39" wide desk. Hold the rails up one at a time and mark their hole locations. This is where they contact the front and rear stiffeners. Pre-drill them with a 3/16" bit. Fasten them on their marks with 3" screws. Slide the drawer in place, connect the drawer glide hardware, and you are done.

Bottom View of Shallow Drawer

THE TUB STACKER

The tub stacker will hold two file tubs as loose drawers. Two tubs hold a lot of files! This unit will fit easily under most desks and tables. If you can not buy a short file cabinet that fits; this is for you! Two of these tub stackers will easily fit under the large desk in chapter seven. This is not realistic for the transverse desk in chapter eight however, because of knee space requirements. But, two tub stackers could fit side by side on the opposite end of the loft bed.

Tub Stacker in Use

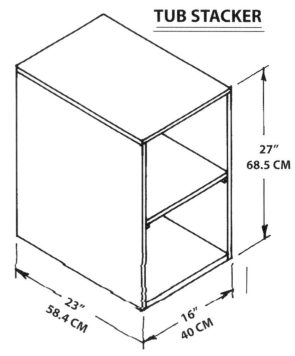

Building the tub stacker is pretty easy. There are not many components, and the fastening is simple. It is made from 1 x 24 edge glued pine (19 mm x 61 cm). Plywood works too, but the exposed edges must be veneered for appearance.

There are two identical sides to make, two identical shelves, plus a top and a back. The shelf cleats are the same small wood rips (blind stop) used through out this book. Each piece must be accurately cut, as everything shows. The edges can be rounded or left square. It should all be sanded smooth and finished.

I like to cut these sorts of pieces on my table saw. Straight, square, and parallel are easily achieved on such a machine. Acceptable results can be accomplished with a portable circular saw, however. The measuring and layout must be more careful, and a guide bar must be used. A saw guide is nothing more than a straight edge clamped to the work piece. The bed of the tool rides against it to accomplish a straight cut. This will produce better quality than simply following a pencil line with your eyes. The distance from the saw blade to the riding edge of the saw bed must be accounted for on the work piece measurement to align the straight edge correctly.

Clamping a Saw Guide

TUB STACKER

SIDE PANEL

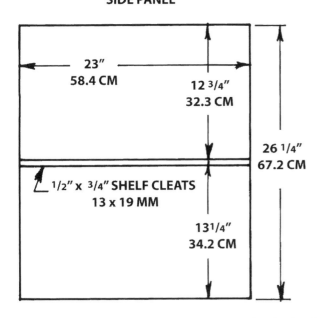

23"
58.4 CM

12 3/4"
32.3 CM

26 1/4"
67.2 CM

1/2" x 3/4" SHELF CLEATS
13 x 19 MM

13 1/4"
34.2 CM

Start by cutting everything to length. Then, rip everything to the correct width. Plane or sand the edges smooth. Next, mark the shelf cleat locations on the side panels. Make a small "x" on both sides of the line. I also make an "x" where the bottom shelf goes. This helps to keep top and bottom properly oriented.

Attach the shelf cleats with a thin bead of wood glue, and temporarily hold in place with spring clamps. Drive four 1" brads in each to permanently secure. If you layout and build, both sides together, the shelves will end up parallel.

Attaching a Shelf Cleat

When both sides are ready, attach the bottom shelf to the first side with a thin bead of construction adhesive and some six penny finish nails (50 mm). Drive them straight! Next, attach the second side panel to the bottom shelf. If any glue squeezes out, be sure to wipe it off completely with a damp cloth while it is still wet.

Now rotate the entire assembly and attach the top panel. You must be sure to place it on top of the side panels, and not between them. Glue one end and nail it, and then the other. Next, install the middle shelf. You need to apply the glue to the sides before inserting the shelf. A couple of spring clamps wedged behind it, helps hold it in position, while you nail it permanently. Six penny finish nails are okay for this too. Address any squeezed out glue before it dries.

Finally, flip it on its front, and attach the back panel. This will maintain its shape permanently. No glue is needed, but lots of four penny box nails are used (40 mm). First get one edge correct, aligning the corners. When that is nailed, push the adjacent side into alignment and nail the far corner to hold it there. Check all sides and corners and nail it off.

I said it was easy. Just a little hand sanding and some varnish and it is ready to use.

THE OVER SIZE CRATE

The oversize crate is basically a 16" cube (40.5 cm) with handles. A pair of these should hold a week's worth of something. They are made from thin plywood panels and cable zip ties. They hold lot, and are easy to make.

To build them, start by cutting up some ¼" (7 mm) luan plywood. Pine or fir are acceptable choices too. I really like the micro-layered Baltic Birch, though it is expensive. Whichever you buy; it must have all voids filled! I also pick them for a light color.

Each cube requires five pieces of ¼" plywood (7 mm) that are 16" square (40.5 cm). A single 4' x 8' sheet of plywood can yield 18 pieces that size. I under size them about a ¹/₁₆" (2 mm) to avoid waste. A new plywood blade, set shallow, will produce the best cutting results. A sharp brad spur drill bit should make the lacing holes cleanly. A 1" diameter hole saw (25 mm) and a coping saw works for the handles. See detail drawing.

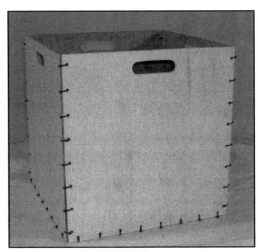

Completed Crate

CRATE DETAILS

BOTTOM VIEW

16"
40 CM

1/4" PLYWOOD
7 MM

16"
40 CM

7/16" PLYWOOD
11 MM

2"
5 CM

TYP.

1"
2.5 CM

MAKE ONE

All five panels can be drilled at one time. Bundle them together, with all four edges flush, and secure with masking tape. Orient their top edges together. Put the bottom panel at the bottom of the pile. Use a sacrifice board to minimize tear-out when the drill bit goes through the bottom piece. Measure and mark the lacing holes, for all three sides. See photo. When you complete the third side, remove the tape and extract the bottom panel. Lay out its fourth side, and drill those too. Deburr the holes where necessary, with a sharp countersink bit and sandpaper.

Drilling Lacing Holes

To make the handle; hold your tape measure in the approximate position, and apply some wide masking tape along side. Mark the hole centers on that, per drawing. Bore with 1" hole saw (25 mm) halfway through, at both centers, and turn the piece over. Bore through the other side of both centers. This method makes a nice clean cut. It only works one piece at a time though. You can't bundle them for this. Next, draw the lines connecting the tangents of the two holes you just made. This should form a 1" x 4½" (25 mm x 10 cm) oblong hole. This connecting section must be cut out with a coping saw. Loosen one end of the saw blade, thread it through the 1" hole, and reconnect. Saw out both lines, and remove the blade again. Set aside. Remove the masking tape from the work piece, and dress up the cut with 100# sandpaper. Make it smooth. Don't leave any rough spots or slivers. Remember, this is a handle! Make a handle for each of the side panels. Sand all the cut edges smooth, for all the panels while you are at it. The rubber sanding block will help to produce straight edges.

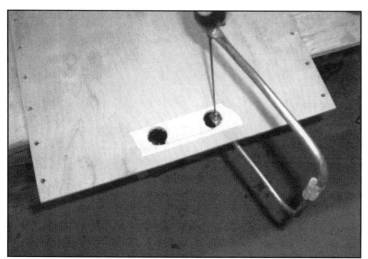

Cutting Handle Slots

CRATE DETAILS

SIDE PANEL

6 1/2"
16 CM

3 1/2"
9 CM

6 1/2"
16 CM

1" x 4 1/2" SLOT
2.5 x 11.5 CM

16"
40 CM

1/4" 0 HOLES

16"
40 CM

MAKE FOUR

Begin assembling with 3 zip ties per side, leaving them very loose. Lay the bottom panel on your work bench first, with one edge over hanging a little. Place a side panel on top of it, and lace its bottom edge to the over hanging bottom edge. Rotate the whole thing 90 degrees, and flop that first side over on its face, off the bottom panel. Now place the second side panel on top of the bottom panel, and lace its bottom edge to the over hanging edge. Now stand it up, and also the first side panel. Lace their vertical corner together with 3 zip ties. See photos. Repeat this procedure for the third and fourth sides.

Lacing the First Edge

Lacing a Vertical Edge

Begin snugging up the bottom edge, working your way around the assembly. Keep the side panels uniformly around the bottom panel, and not on it. Then snug up the vertical corners. These should just meet, not lap over each other's end grain. See photo. When everything is properly positioned and snugged up tight, go ahead and lace up the rest of the holes. Make them all tight. Trim off the excess with a wire cutters or tin snip.

That completes the assembly. You can either varnish them, or leave them "raw". I don't recommend an oil finish for these; it could transfer to your contents.

THE WOODEN UTILITY BOX

To build the wooden box you will need to cut your boards to length, glue and nail them together, attach the blind stops to the bottom edge, and fit a plywood panel inside. Some rope handles completes the package. This one is sized to fit the bottom space of the shelf cabinet in chapter ten. You could make the size almost anything, within limits. The following material list calls for 1 x 12 (19 x 286 mm) pine boards for the sides. Plywood rips; ³/₄" thick (19 mm) are an acceptable substitute.

Completed Utility Box

Material list

> 1 – 1x 12 x 10', # 2 pine (19 x 286 mm x 3 m)
> 1 – ¹/₄" plywood panel; 14¹/₂" x 36¹/₂" min.
>   (7 mm x 37 cm x 92.6 cm)
> 1 – ¹/₂" x ³/₄" blind stop x 9' (12 x 18 mm x 3 m)
> 16 – 8d finish nails (60 mm)
> 30 – 1" brads (25 mm)
> 1 – small bottle wood glue
> 1 – 12 oz. tube construction adhesive (.35 liter)
> ³/₈" rope x 8' long (10 mm x 3 m)

The long boards can be cut in half for transport. When you get them to your work area, cut the 1 x 12 (19 x 286 mm) to length for the sides. You need two pieces at 38" long (96.5 cm) and two pieces at 14¹/₂" long (37 cm). You can easily make one of each, from a five footer (1.5 m). Cut your blind stop to 14¹/₂" pieces (37 cm) and 35¹/₂" pieces (90 cm), same concept. Cut your plywood panel to size also. I usually undersize that piece about ¹/₁₆" in both dimensions (2 mm) to make the assembly easier and faster. (14⁷/₁₆" x 36⁷/₁₆" or 36.7 cm x 92.5 cm).

Attach the long cleats (blind stop) to the long sides. Apply a thin bead of wood glue to the bottom, inner face, of the long board first. Then put them together. Hold their edges and ends flush. Temporarily hold them with clamps, while you drive the brads to permanently fasten them. Do both long sides likewise.

Next, apply a thin bead of wood glue to the end grain of a short side. Turn this board up on edge with the glued end toward you, and the other

UTILITY BOX
SECTION VIEW

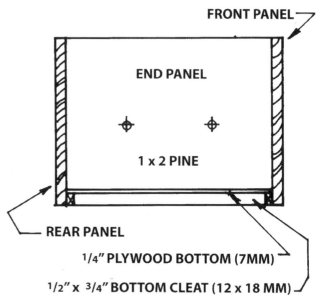

FRONT PANEL

END PANEL

1 x 2 PINE

REAR PANEL

1/4" PLYWOOD BOTTOM (7MM)

1/2" x 3/4" BOTTOM CLEAT (12 x 18 MM)

Attaching Cleats

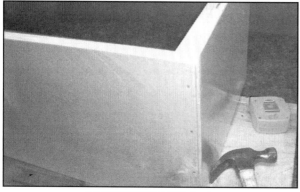

Assembling Front and Side Panels

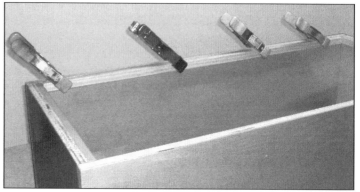

Attaching Bottom Cleats

against a wall. (Doing this on a work bench is easier than the floor.) Place the front side board in position with it to form the first corner. Keeping the cleat down, and the edges flush; drive the top nail into both. Re-check your edges for flush, and drive the bottom nail. Move to other the end, and attach the second short side in the same way. Rotate the assembly 180 degrees and attach the back side board in the same way. Work your way around, filling in all those middle nails. When they are all driven, set them all properly.

Now, flip the assembly up on edge, with the bottom toward you. Apply a thin bead of wood glue to the bottom portion of the inner face, of the short side. Place the blind stop in position, and secure with clamps. Nail it off with more brads. Keep the spacing about 8"or less (20 cm). Repeat for the last side.

Lay the assembly back down, and trial fit the bottom panel. You may have to wrack the assembly into a square shape to fit. You

Securing the bottom Panel

may even have to sand a little off the panel edges. When you are sure it fits, apply a 1/8" (4 mm) bead of construction adhesive to the top surface of the blind stop, the entire perimeter. Set the panel down into it, and hold with something heavy until the adhesive sets up.

Making Rope Handles

While you are waiting for the glue to cure, measure and mark the rope handle hole locations, on all four sides. Drill them all out ½" diameter (13 mm). Use sharp drill bit for this and make nice clean holes. Deburr if necessary. Cut your rope into 2' pieces now (61 cm). If this is a course twisted rope, you must wrap some electrical tape around the area to be cut prior to cutting. This will prevent unraveling during the process. If you tape up a 2" portion (50 mm) and cut the center of it, you have two preserved ends. Most braided ropes will be ok as is. Insert both ends in their holes, pull the ends through an equal amount to form the handle. Hold a comfortable hand space on the handle side, and tie an overhand knot on the back side, for each rope end. Rub a generous amount of wood glue into the knot and a couple inches after it. Make all four handles likewise. When the applied glue is good and dry, trim off the excess rope. Apply a little more glue to the fresh cut end. This should keep them from unraveling.

The box is now complete. You can varnish it, or you can leave it raw.

CD STORAGE SLOTS

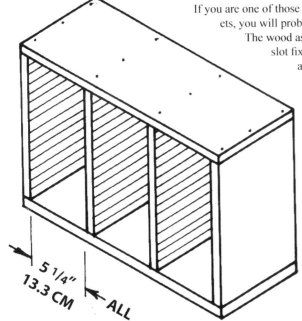

If you are one of those people who absolutely must keep their CDs, in the original hard plastic jackets, you will probably want this. This is both useful, and easily made; a great beginner project! The wood assembly will fit on a shelf, desk, floor space, etc. It uses prefabricated plastic slot fixtures,(available at woodworker supply store) to hold the CD cases. These attach to the wood sides with short screws. Each bank of slots holds 20 CDs, so the double wide contains 40, and the triple wide contains 60. If your collection is greater than that, perhaps another storage type would serve you better. (See chapter thirteen.)

5 1/4"
13.3 CM ← ALL

Both configurations shown are designed to be simple construction. Standard width boards are cut to length with square cuts. Edges are slightly rounded with sandpaper. Assembly is square and flush using wood glue and finish nails. The only assembly layout required is for the wood partitions. The plastic slots must be attached to the sides prior to assembly. Note how they flush the front edges of the wood. I do recommend varnishing this. The back panel should be a light colored plywood and varnished both sides. If this will work for you; copy the appropriate material list and purchase the necessary materials.

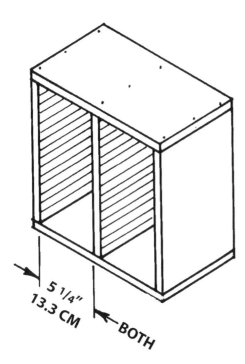

Material list for the double wide

1 – 1 x 8 x 6', #2 pine (19 x 184 mm x 1.8 m)
1 – ¼" plywood scrap; 13" x 14" min. (7 mm x 33 cm x 35.5 cm)
16 – 8d finish nails (60 mm)
24 – 2d box nails (25 mm)
2 – pairs of plastic CD slot fixture
1 – small bottle wood glue

Cutting list for the double wide

3 – 1 x 8 x 12⅝" long (19 x 184 mm x 32.2 cm)
2 – 1 x 8 x 12⅝" long (19 x 184 mm x 31.5 cm)
1 – ¼" plywood panel at 12¾" x 14" ((7 mm x 32.5 cm x 35.5 cm)

Material list for the triple wide

1 – 1 x 8 x 8', #2 pine (19 x 184 mm x 2.4 m)
1 – ¼" plywood scrap; 13" x 19" min. (7 mm x 33 cm x 48 cm)
20 – 8d finish nails (60 mm)
30 – 2d box nails (25 mm)
3 – pairs of plastic CD slot
    fixture
1 – small bottle wood glue

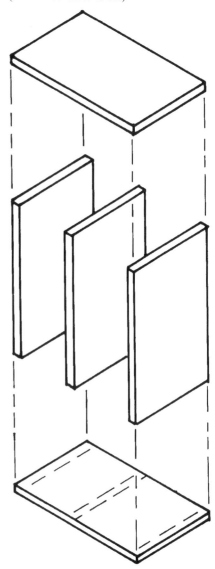

Cutting list for the triple wide

4 – 1 x 8 x 12⅝" long (19 x 184 mm x 32.2 cm)
2 – 1 x 8 x 18¾" long (19 x 184 mm x 47.5 cm)
1 – ¼" plywood panel at 12¾" x 18¾" (7 mm x 32.5 cm x 47.5 cm)

Cut your boards to size, whichever model you are building. Pre-drill the nail starter holes in both ends of the top and bottom boards. Sand everything smooth, especially the edges. Dust off everything. Make a small pencil mark on each side that receives a plastic slot fixture. You will notice they are made left and right. Only remove them from the package and install them in pairs, together. Keep their front edges flush, or at least the same. Secure with small screws.

Attaching Plastic Slots to Side Panels

Next, assemble the four perimeter boards. Don't forget a light bead of wood glue on the end grain of the side pieces before nailing the top and bottom to them. Just do the two outer nails for now. Carefully measure and mark the partition locations. Carefully slide them in and fasten them on their marks. It works best to do them one at a time. Trial fit a CD in each of the banks as you go, to ensure they are all correctly spaced. Nail all the front edges first, and then the back edges. When you are ready, apply the back panel. Wrack the cabinet into shape if you must. You cut the panel square, so make the cabinet shape fit it. Start on one side, hold the edge and ends flush, and nail it off. Start the first nail an inch from the corner and every couple inches from there. Then wrack to fit and tack an opposite corner. Nail the whole back side perimeter. Drive those nails straight! Set the finish nails, apply wood putty to them, and sand to appearance grade. Varnish the wood as before.

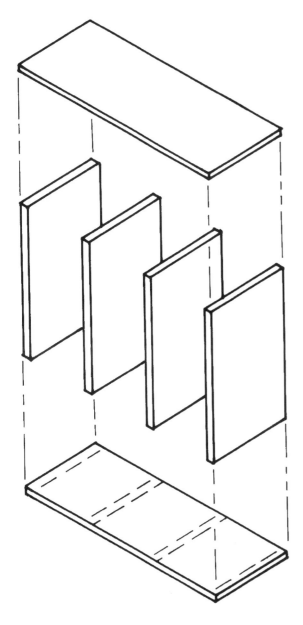

Assembling Perimeter Panels and Back

Installing Partition Panels

You are done! It works, it matches, and its cool!

CHAPTER TWELVE

CLOTHES HANGING; I, II, & III

Clothes, Option I

If your dorm, apartment, or bedroom doesn't have adequate closet space, the ideas in this chapter could really enhance your quality of life. Option I, shown in the photo, is mounted under the mattress rail. It has a single closet rod, 42" long (107 cm). Options II & III are mounted outside the bed frame on the unused end. I say unused, because you will not be able to use that end frame as a ladder with the closet rod attached there. You also need a few feet of space from walls or furniture for this. Option II has a single closet rod 39" long (99 cm) plus a shelf. Option III has two rods and two shelves. See photos. The double rod and shelf setup will hold twice as many clothes, but not the really long stuff, basically just shirt length. This should work for most of your clothes. Additionally, both options II & III, can be built with wire

Clothes, Option III

shelving. I also recommend adding a sturdy robe hook near each end of your loft bed. Fasten securely to the 2 x 8 (38 x 184 mm) mattress rail. A third hook

Clothes, Option II

at half the height could hold your backpack, gym bag, etc. If you decide that one or more of these options is in your future, copy the appropriate material list and go shopping.

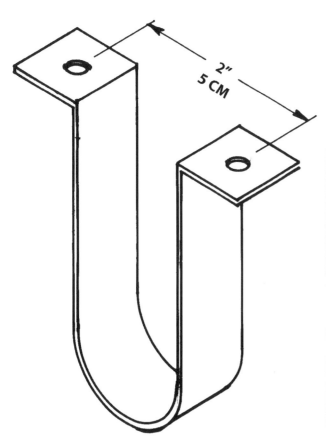

2"
5 CM

To build option I, you need some fir closet rod, and some heavy gauge strapping, plus some screws. Begin by cutting to length the strapping for your custom made support brackets. Then lay out the holes and bend locations, as per detail drawing. A medium point marker is good for this. Center punch the holes to prevent the drill bit from wandering. It helps to put a drop or two of oil on the drill bit when going through metal. Repeat at least once per hole. Be sure to remove any burrs left from drilling or cutting. File, grind, countersink them, whatever it takes.

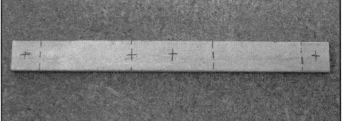

Layout of Holes and Bends

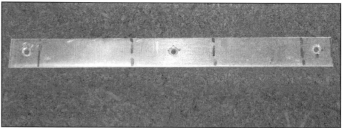

Strapping with Holes

Next make the two ninety degree bends. A sturdy vise and a medium size hammer will make this part easy. Just clamp it up leaving the lay out mark about $^1/_{16}$" past the vise jaw edge (2 mm). Pound it over until you have a nice square corner. Repeat for the

Bending Mounting Tabs

other one, making sure the direction of bend is correct. When both mounting ears are formed, turn the piece over, and forcefully wrap it around your closet rod until it assumes the correct "U" shape. See photograph. It helps to step on the closet rod while you do this. This takes some effort, but it is not insurmountable. You will need to make two of these. They must be identical. A short length of 1"

Forming U-Bend over Closet Rod

(25 mm) steel pipe clamped in the vice makes an even better forming jig.

If you don't have access to a vise, you will have a harder job to form those mounting ears. It can be done with two large pliers, or even by pounding over the edge of some scrap iron.

UNDERMOUNT BRACKET

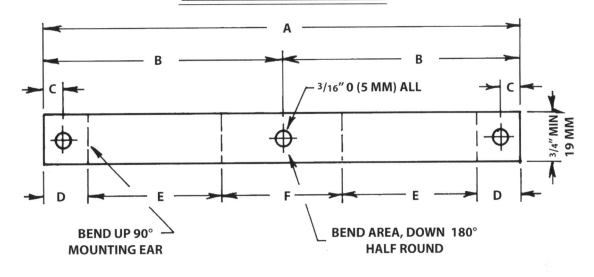

3/16" 0 (5 MM) ALL

3/4" MIN / 19 MM

BEND UP 90°
MOUNTING EAR

BEND AREA, DOWN 180°
HALF ROUND

A	B	C	D	E	F
8"	4"	3/8"	3/4"	2 1/4"	2"
20 CM	10 CM	1 CM	2 CM	5.5 CM	5 CM

MAKE FROM HEAVY STRAPPING

Next, cut the closet rod to 42" long (107 cm). Slightly round the sharp edges on both ends, using your 100# sandpaper.

OPTION I

MOUNTING HOLE LOCATIONS

Now you must choose which end of the under story space you will attach these to. Measure and mark 9" and 11" (23 cm and 30.5 cm) along the bottom edge of the mattress rail. See drawing. Square across the rail's edge, and mark the hole locations centered. Drill 1/8" pilot holes (3 mm). Repeat this for the other mattress rail. Next, attach your custom made brackets to these two locations using 2" (50 mm) pan head screws. Finally, fit your closet rod in place. Mark and drill pilot holes in each end, corresponding to the brackets. Secure with ¾" (19 mm) pan head screws. Option I is ready to hang clothes!

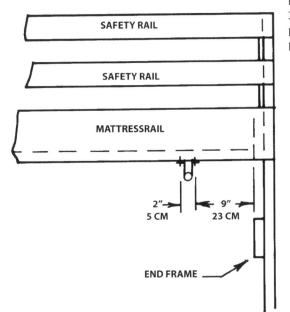

SAFETY RAIL

SAFETY RAIL

MATTRESSRAIL

2"
5 CM

9"
23 CM

END FRAME

Clothes, Option I

If you chose option II, you will need one rod, one 16" wide shelf (40 cm), and two standard rod and shelf brackets, plus a few screws. To get started, you must measure and mark 63" (160 cm) from the floor, on both of the vertical 2 x 6s. This is the back side of the unused end. Next, you make a mark ¾" in from the outside edge (19 mm), crossing that mark. Drill a ⅛" pilot hole at those locations (3 mm) for both of the vertical 2 x 6s. Then drive a 1½" (38 mm) pan head screw into each, leaving about ¼" sticking out (7 mm). Now you can slip the rod and shelf bracket over the screws and tighten them. You will notice that the brackets have a keyhole slot for this.

OPTION II

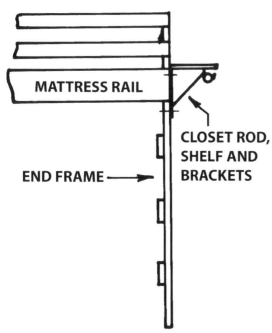

MATTRESS RAIL

CLOSET ROD, SHELF AND BRACKETS

END FRAME ———▶

OPTION II

MOUNTING HOLE LOCATIONS

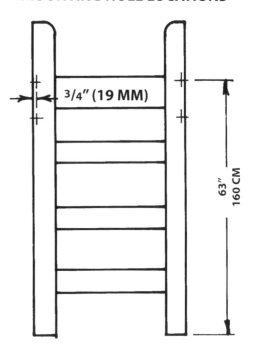

3/4" (19 MM)

63" / 160 CM

Clothes, Option II

Now adjust the bottom edge of the bracket plumb, or a uniform edge distance, and fasten it also. This can be drilled in place. Complete both brackets.

Be sure to wear safety glasses when installing these brackets. They are close to eye level. It is pretty easy to turn around and poke yourself in the face with a pointed metal end! Don't risk damaging your eye for a moment's convenience. That would make a poor trade.

Next, you should cut the wooden closet rod to 39" length (99 cm) and the shelf likewise. Hold the rod in place, and mark the holes. Drill pilot holes at both marks. Put the rod back, and fasten with ¾" (19 mm) pan head screws. Now, put the shelf in its place, mark the holes, and pre-drill them. If the brackets appear crooked, correct your marks parallel with the shelf ends before drilling. The screws into the shelf will hold the brackets square, when you are done. Put the shelf back up and screw it tight. That's all there is to it.

To build option III, you will need twice the material of option II, because you are doubling everything. Make your layout marks 37" and 76" from the floor (94 cm and 193 cm). Measure in ¾" from the edges to complete the crosshairs of your mounting hole locations. Pre-drill all four holes. Next, drive in those screws. Leave them sticking out about ¼" (7 mm) as before. Install your lower brackets first, then their closet rod and the narrower shelf. Install the upper brackets next, and the wooden rod, and the wide shelf. (In my opinion, the lower set is better with the narrow shelf, otherwise getting the coat hangers on and off is cumbersome.)

OPTION III

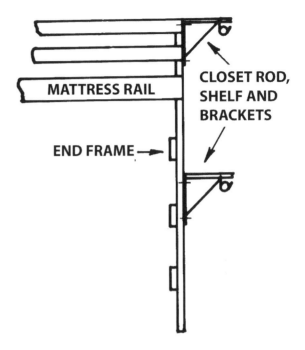

OPTION III

MOUNTING HOLE LOCATIONS

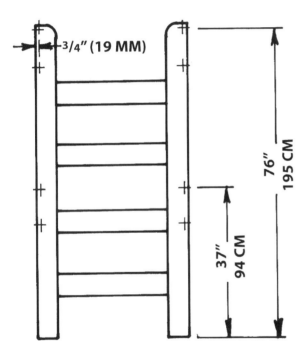

Clothes, Option III

There is still another option, and that is the factory coated wire shelving, with integral coat hanging space. Some people love this stuff. It looks modern and doesn't collect much dust. It is quite versatile in application, and easy to install. It is fairly durable. The cost is a little more. The biggest difference for the installer lies in the cutting method. A wire cutter, a bolt cutter, and a hacksaw are needed. All the cut ends will get rubber or plastic covers to protect your clothes and skin.

Welded Wire Shelving

If you were to adapt option III for wire shelving, substitute the attached material list when shopping. The additional 2 x 4 must be cut to 77½" long (197 cm) and attached midway between the other two, and plumb. See drawing.

The layout marks are at 38" and 77½" high (97 cm and 197 cm). This reflects the top of the shelf, instead of the mounting holes themselves. You will have to work downwards from the shelf height. Attach all the plastic "back" brackets, at the shelf height. Then cut your shelving to 38½" long (98 cm). The end covers will increase the length a little. Hang the shelf on the "back" brackets. Attach the angle braces next. Make sure the shelf is level, or ninety degrees from plumb. Fasten with screws. Most of the angle brackets sold have little tabs you can bend over the shelf rod to permanently attach them. Make sure to install any end protectors on wires or rods. If you attached everything securely, any of these options should serve you well for a long time.

Closet rod brackets, like doorknobs and latches, are considered builder's hardware. They can actually be attached to the walls of your closet or bedroom (assuming you have permission). Sometimes, upgrading the existing storage is the most practical solution. The bracket height dimensions previously given are the current standard. Obviously, they must be secured to the wall studs. You can't count on plaster or drywall bearing their weight. Shelves should be installed level, even if the floors are not. You would have to measure the space you have and buy the appropriate lengths and quantities of material. Most home improvement stores have a whole section for this, and many sample layouts. This is loosely termed "closet enhancement". The more options you have to choose from, the more resourceful your solutions can be. Avoid the million dollar ideas. You probably won't live there long enough to justify the cost. Practical is good, and appearance matters, too. Choose well. Best of luck to you.

...OR MAKE BUNK BEDS!

It may be that some readers will need to make bunk beds to maximize their dwelling space. These will stack two bed platforms in the same floor space. This chapter has two distinctly different designs: one is child size, and the other is adult size. Since the smaller bodies of children have different needs and abilities than young adults, these two designs accommodate those particular differences.

The U.S. government regulations state different dimensions and configuration for children than for adults. For starters, no child under age six may be allowed on an upper bunk of any kind! (This means 30" or more above the floor). The ladder rungs must be closer together, the guard rails configured a little differently, and the maximum platform height above the floor is less. The regulations and guidelines allow adult beds to be taller, their ladder rungs may be farther apart, and generally assume a higher level of coordination and dexterity by their intended user. They do not seem to distinguish an age or size difference for choking and entrapment hazards. Both of these designs, and the loft beds, endeavor to eliminate those.

Like all the other accessory options, I recommend you read it through, evaluate your actual needs, and make your choices.

THE CHILD SIZE BUNK BED

This design is extrapolated from a standard twin size mattress, 38" x 75" (97 cm x 190 cm). Although the methods and materials are identical to the other bed frames in the preceding chapters, the proportions are scaled back to a child's size. The ladder rungs are only 12" apart (30.5 cm). The upper platform height is only 48" (122 cm), and the foot rail is notched for safer use by a child. This bed swaps some dog leg gussets for the diagonal braces. The gussets eliminate one of the entrapment hazards, while preserving structural integrity. If this bed fits your needs, copy the material lists, make the necessary purchases, and let's build something!

Material list

    4 – 2 x 6 x 6' SPF (38 x 140 mm x 1.8 m)
    6 – 2 x 8 x 8' SPF (38 x 184 mm x 1.8 m)
    6 – 2 x 4 x 8' SPF (38 x 89 mm x 1.8 m)
    4 – 2 x 2 x 8' SPF (38 x 38 mm x 1.8 m)
    1 – 1 x 8 x 4' SPF (19 x 184 mm x 1.25 m)
    1 – 1 x 24" x 60" edge glued pine (19 mm x 61 cm x 152 cm)
    1 – 1 x 18" x 48" edge glued pine (19 mm x 46 cm x 1.25 m)
    16 – $^5/_{16}$" x 4" lag screws (8 mm x 10 cm)
    16 – $^5/_{16}$" flat washers (8mm)
    1# – 3" course thread screws (80 mm)
    1# – 2½" course thread screws (65 mm)
    1# – 2" course thread screws (50 mm)
    1 – 12 oz. tube construction adhesive (.35 liter)
    2 – ¼" x 4' flat loop chain (7 mm x 1.25 m)
    3 – 1¼" wafer head screws (30 mm)
    8 – 11" zip ties (28 cm)

Cutting list

    2 x 6 x 61-1/2" lg. (38 x 140 mm x 156 cm)
    4 – 2 x 8 x 82" lg. (38 x 184 mm x 208 cm)
    2 – 2 x 8 x 39" lg. (38 x 184 mm x 99 cm)
    2 x 6 x 39" lg. (38 x 140 mm x 99 cm)
    4 – 2 x 4 x 82" lg. (38 x 89 mm x 208 cm)
    4 – 2 x 4 x 39" lg. (38 x 89 mm x 99 cm)
    4 – 2 x 2 x 76" lg. (38 x 38 x 193 cm)
    2 – 2 x 4 x 14" lg. (from scrap) (38 x 89 mm x 35.5 cm)
    2 – 2 x 4 x 12" lg. (from scrap) (38 x 89 mm x 30 cm)

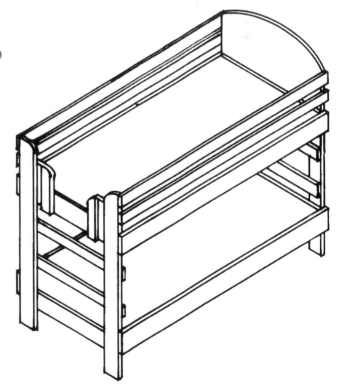

BRACING GUSSET DETAIL

MAKE ONE LEFT, ONE RIGHT

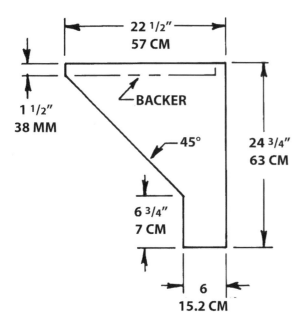

22 1/2"
57 CM

BACKER

1 1/2"
38 MM

45°

24 3/4"
63 CM

6 3/4"
7 CM

6
15.2 CM

**MAKE FROM 1 x 24 EDGE GLUED PINE
ROUND OVER ALL EDGES, BOTH SIDES
(19 MM x 61 CM)**

1 – 1 x 8 x 39" lg. (19 x 184 mm x 99 cm)
1 – 1 x 18" x 39" lg. shaped per drawing (19mm x 46 cm x 99 cm)
2 – 1 x 24" gussets, per drawing (19 mm x 61 cm)

Cut all your boards to length and shape. Check them off your list as you go. Note the gusset details, and the arched upper headboard. This is the same headboard found in chapter one. When all the parts are cut to size and shape, (and planed if necessary); round over all the edges to eliminate any sharp corners. Sand everything uniformly smooth with 100# sandpaper. Please don't forget to work safely! Wear those protective glasses!

Lay out and drill the holes in your 2 x 2 ledgers (38 x 38). Likewise, drill all the holes in the ladder rungs. Assemble the mattress rails from the long 2 x 8s and 2 x 2s (38 x 184 mm and 38 x 38 mm). Secure the ledger with construction adhesive and 2½" screws (65 mm). Keep the end setbacks equal and the bottom edge flush. Move them aside as you complete them.

Next, place all four of the 2 x 6 vertical supports on your saw horses. Line up the ends together. Measure all the rung locations on the 2 x 6s. Consult the drawing. These are 12" (30.5 cm), to the first mark, and each thereafter. Square across each board, and make a small "x" mark on the bottom side of that pencil line. Mark the width of the rung on the board also; that gives you a target for applying the adhesive.

To assemble the end frames, you will need space. Clear out the saw horses, and anything else in the way. Lay two of your marked 2 x 6s (38 x 140 mm), flat on the floor, with their feet touching the wall, about 2' apart (60 cm). Apply a ¼" (7 mm), bead of adhesive, in a ring shape within the top most glue zone of both vertical members. Repeat for the bottom rung, on both also. Now, set the upper and lower rungs in position. Note the size difference, according to the drawing. Hold one on its marks, with the end flush, and drive in the first 2½" screw (65 mm). Don't sink

A	B	C	D
39"	77½"	16"	64"
99 CM	197 CM	40.5 CM	162.5 CM

2 x 6 = 38 x 140 MM

2 x 8 = 38 x 184 MM

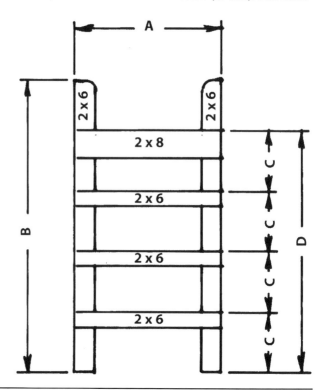

A

2 x 6   2 x 6

2 x 8

2 x 6

C

2 x 6

C

B   2 x 6   C   D

C

the screw, just make it snug. Now fasten the other end the same way, and then repeat for the other rung. Measure across the diagonals and adjust the shape for squareness. When the diagonal dimensions are equal, the frame is square. You must work fast, before the adhesive sets up. When you get it right, sink the screws. Re-check, and add the other screws. Attach the intermediate rungs, 2 x 4s (38 x 89 mm), on their marks. Secure them with more adhesive and screws. The second end frame must be assembled identical to the first.

When the adhesive is cured, scrape, gouge, or sand off any excess that squeezed out. Pre-finish all your wood parts, and these large sub-assemblies. Chapter four has step by step instructions for both varnishing and painting. When the finish has dried and cured, you should pre-drill the holes in all the horizontal rails. See drawings.

The on-site assembly follows the same process as the other bed frames. Measure and mark the outer edges of the vertical supports to establish the rail locations. Hold the end frames on edge horizontally, and parallel, about 6' apart (1.8 m). Attach your bottom mattress rail first, with just one screw per end for now. Then attach the upper mattress rail, with just one screw per end also. Measure the diagonals, and adjust the shape square. Add the two triangular gussets now, and re-check for squareness. If it is good, fill in all the missing screws, and sink them. This includes the lag screws. Attach the two safety rails next and fasten with screws.

REAR VIEW ASSEMBLY

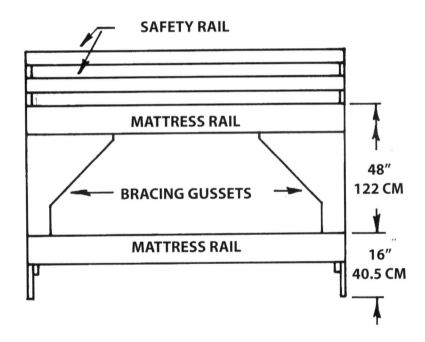

CHILD SIZE BUNK

WITH NOTCHED FOOTRAIL

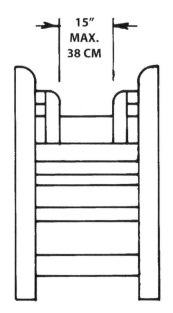

15"
MAX.
38 CM

Now you must ease the assembly up to its normal vertical position. This requires at least two people. Pound some temporary nails just under each of the edge layout marks. These will help you assemble the rails on the open side. Attach the lower mattress rail first, and then the upper one. Check for squareness, and run all the screws in when ready. Put up the safety rails next, and then the head board, and the notched foot rail.

The bed slats are next: be sure to secure them! Spring slats are meant to flex and spring. They also have a way of creeping out of position. The spring slat assembly should be tied to the ledgers on all four corners of the bed frame. If you have flat boards, both ends of every board should be screwed to the ledger. These precautions will prevent a hole or void from opening up and presenting an entrapment hazard. The flat boards should also be fastened across the bottom of the upper mattress rails about mid span. This will restrain the ledgers from ever spreading and allowing the bed slats or mattress to fall through. (This is admittedly a pretty small risk). You are ready for the mattresses, it is built!

THE ADULT SIZE, OR BARRACKS STYLE, BUNK BED

This size bunk bed is designed around an 80" long twin mattress (203 cm). This will include two end frames, four mattress rails, a few safety rails and the headboards. Since this bed has less guard rail height, the vertical supports are cut a little shorter. The head boards are low and straight to match. It has large diagonal braces to ensure stability. These are configured and attached differently than the loft beds. Should you decide to build this, study the following drawings, material list, and cutting list. These lists are for building the bed frame. You will also need two mattresses!

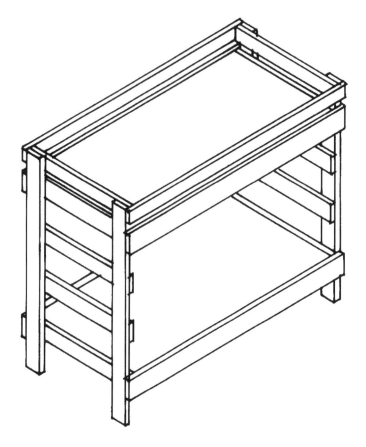

Material list

4 – 2 x 6 x 6' SPF (38 x 140 mm x 1.8 m)
2 – 2 x 6 x 10' SPF (38 x 140 mm x 3 m)
5 – 2 x 8 x 8' SPF (38 x 184 mm x 2.4 m)
4 – 2 x 2 x 8' SPF (38 x 38 mm x 2.4 m)
3 – 2 x 4 x 8' SPF (38 x 89 mm x 2.4 m)
1 – 1 x 8 x 8' #2 pine (19 x 184 mm x 2.4 m)
1 – 1 x 6 x 10' #2 pine (19 x 140 mm x 3 m)
16 – ⁵/₁₆" x 4" lag screws (8 mm x 10 cm)
16 – ⁵/₁₆" flat washers (8 mm)
1# – 3' course thread screws (80 mm)
1# – 2¹/₂" course thread screws (65 mm)
1# – 2" course thread screws (50 mm)
8 – 11" zip ties (28 cm)
1 – 12 oz. tube construction adhesive (.35 liter)

Cutting list

4 – 2 x 6 x 70¾" lg. (38 x 140 mm x 180 cm)
6 – 2 x 6 x 39"lg. (38 x 140 mm x 99 cm)
2 – 2 x 8 x 39" lg. (38 x 184 mm x 99 cm)
4 – 2 x 8 x 86" lg. (38 x 184 mm x 218.5 cm)
2 – 2 x 4 x 86" lg. (38 x 89 mm x 218.5 cm)
1 – 2 x 4 x 39" lg. (38 x 89 mm x 99 cm)
2 – 1 x 8 x 39" lg. (19 x 184 mm x 99 cm)
2 – 1 x 6 x 51" lg. angle cut braces (19 x 140 mm x 130 cm)
2 – 1 x 10 x 8" angle filler (19 x 240 mm x 20 cm)
2 – 1 x 6 x 10" backer (19 x 140 mm x 28 cm)

Cut all your boards to length and shape, checking them off
your list as you go. Plane the cuts smooth if you need to.
Round over all the edges, to eliminate any sharp corners, and
sand out everything uniformly smooth with 100# sandpaper.
Don't forget to practice safe work habits!

Attach the first 2 x 2 ledger (38 x 38 mm), to a 2 x 8 mattress rail (38 x 184 mm), with construction adhesive and 2½"
screws (65 mm). Keep the end set backs equal and the bottom
edges flush. Repeat for the remaining three mattress rails. Set
them aside when they are done.

Next you must assemble the two end frames. These are large,
and require a lot of space for the process. You also must work
fast once you spread the adhesive. Begin by laying out the
rung locations on the faces of the 2 x 6 (38 x 140 mm), vertical
supports. You can do this on top of the saw horses fairly easy.
Mark all four vertical members, then clear some working space
and get ready.

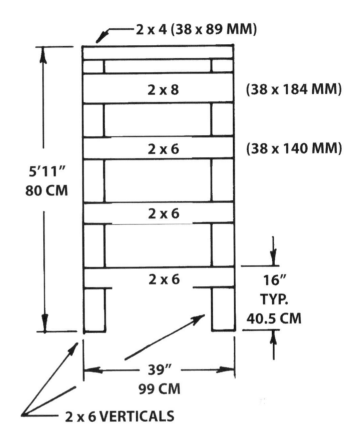

END FRAME ASSEMBLY

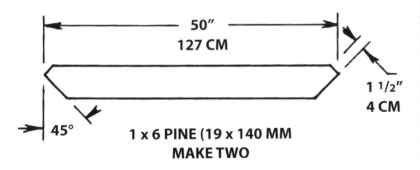

ANGLE BRACE DETAIL

Set two of the 2 x 6 vertical supports flat on the
ground with their feet against a wall, (or heavy
board), and about 2' apart (60 cm). They should be
parallel, with the marks up! Apply a ¼" (7 mm),
bead of adhesive in a large circular pattern in both
of the top rung locations on the vertical supports. (If
you marked both edges of the rung locations, it will
be easy to stay within the marks). Note the rung size
difference in the drawing. Now place the top rung
in position, sandwiching the adhesive. Hold it on its
marks, with the end flush, and drive in a 2½" screw
(65 mm). Don't sink it, just make it snug. Repeat this
procedure for the other end of the top rung. Next, apply adhesive to the bottom rung locations, and place
a 2 x 6 rung there. Hold it on its marks, with the end
flush, and drive in one screw, as before. Repeat for
the other end of the rung. Square up this square up

this frame by measuring diagonally, and adjusting the shape until those measurements are equal. Re-check
your measurements after you tighten or add another fastener. Fill in the missing screws, and sink them too. Add the intermediate rungs and
secure with more adhesive and screws. Repeat this entire procedure for the second end frame. When the adhesive is cured out hard; scrape
or sand off any excess that squeezed out.

Prefabricate the two brace fillers according to the drawing. Make one left and one right.

BRACE FILLER DETAIL

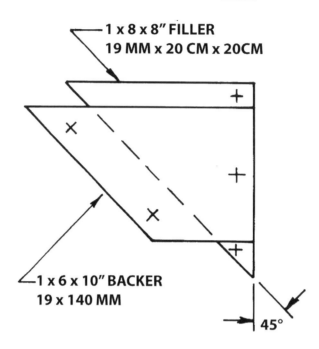

1 x 8 x 8" FILLER
19 MM x 20 CM x 20CM

1 x 6 x 10" BACKER
19 x 140 MM

45°

MAKE ONE LEFT, ONE RIGHT
LAMINATE WITH ADHESIVE

Pre-finish all these wood surfaces before the final onsite assembly. Chapter four has step by step instructions for both varnishing and painting. When the chosen finish is dry and cured, mark all the hole locations on all of your rails and bracing, per detail drawing. Drill all the holes prior to transporting the bed frame to its user destination.

Bring all the bed frame parts into the room it will be used in. Don't crowd yourself with other belongings yet; erecting this requires some room to maneuver. You need a helper for this. (At least one can hold while the other fastens). Lay out all the rail locations on the edges of your end frames now. Set the two end frames horizontally, and on edge, with their feet against a wall, about 7' apart (2.1 m). Now lay the first mattress rail in the lowest position. Make the edges flush, hold it on its marks, and drive one 3" (80 mm), screw in each end. Remember, just snug for now. Attach the center wood bracket to the lower edge of the next rail to be used.

Now, attach that second mattress rail in the top position. Hold it against the rung, and matching the edges. Secure with a 3" (80 mm), screw on each end. You now have a very loose parallelogram. Measure diagonally and adjust the shape for squareness. If you hold the feet tight against the wall, only the tops need move right or left to adjust. When it looks right, or equal, put in a diagonal brace. Re-check your measurement. If everything still looks good, put on the other brace. Re-check again. Fill in all the missing screws now, including the lags. Go ahead and attach the safety rail now, while it can be easily reached and then the two brace fillers.

Ease the entire assembly into its normal vertical position. Use your legs, and spare your back! Pound in some temporary nails, 8d sinkers (60 mm), just under the edge lay out marks to support the mattress rails while you finish assembling. Set a mattress rail in the bottom position. Hold it tightly against the end frame. Secure it with one 3" screw (80 mm). Repeat this for the other end. Next, hoist the last mattress rail into position. Hold it tight to its marks and drive a screw in each end. Measure diagonally. You can still rack it and correct a lean at this point. If it looks square (diagonally equal), go ahead and run in all your 3" screws. Drive the lag screws as well. Put the safety rail up next, and secure with two 3" screws for each end. The two head boards can go on next. Fasten them with 2" screws (50 mm). The upper bunk gets a foot rail, too.

REAR VIEW ASSEMBLY

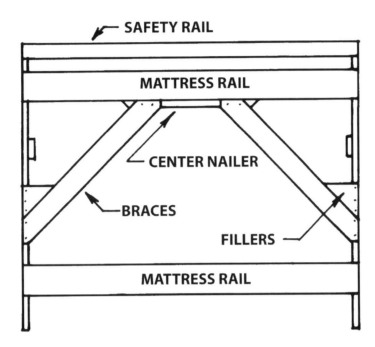

The bed slats can go in now. Work from the top down to maximize your productivity. These must be secured with screws or ties to prevent them creeping out of position. (Movement could create a void or entrapment hazard). The restrainer chain is next. Attach it across the bottom of the upper mattress rails, about mid span. This will prevent the ledgers from ever spreading. The mattresses go in last. That's it then. You are done!

CHAPTER FOURTEEN

MORE RESOURCES

This chapter describes other things, (resources), to store your belongings. Some work with this loft bed system. Some stand alone, meaning they would work with or without it. This assumes, of course, that you already have a list and growing assortment of consumable supplies to maintain health and hygiene of yourself, and the apartment. Either of those could generate a book unto itself.

Storage needs only seem to increase with time. It gets critical when you down size to a smaller space. For example; where do you keep those seasonal clothes in the off season? Sporting goods are typically bulky, and some require air drying between uses. How numerous is your CD collection at this time? Or the paper flow you generate, how much to keep, and for how long? I would hope that this chapter will give you a few more ideas to manage these things.

Various File Tubs

Clear plastic file boxes, with snap-on lids. These basically come in four sizes: 13½" wide x 6" long, 13½" wide x 10½" long, 13½" wide x 17¾" long, and 13½" wide x 22¾" long, (34 cm x 15 cm, or 27 cm, or 45 cm, or 58 cm). They fit the open shelves in chapter ten nicely. They also stack well under a desk. There isn't anything that says you actually have to keep files in them either! You could store socks, or underwear, or whatever you want. These are very handy. You can find them at office supply stores.

Utility tubs with lids are sold in many sizes; 16 gallon, 18 gallon, 20 gallon, 22 gallon, etc., (60 liter, 70 liter, 80 liter, 90 liter). These are very sturdy and durable. They are usually opaque, or colored plastic, so labeling is more important than with clear tubs. Most of these have a wide overhanging flange to support the lid, which wastes some space. These are sold at discount retailers and home improvement centers.

Plastic drawer stacks come in a variety sizes. They are good to store paper reams, craft supplies, etc. They are too small for clothes. Most are not sturdy enough for files or books. They are sold at office stores and discount retailers.

A two drawer file cabinet will easily fit under the desk top in chapter 7. Some are made of sheet metal, some are wood, and some are particle board. These are great for files, spare reams of paper. You can find these at office stores and discount retailers.

Cheap metal book ends come in a few sizes. They help hold things upright at the beginning of the season, when your shelf, file tub, etc. is mostly empty. These are very useful and durable. They are sold at office supply stores and discount retailers.

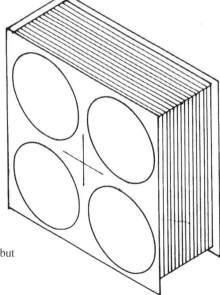

CDs and DVDs can be stored a variety of ways. There are different sizes, or capacities, of wallets and albums made for this. While they only store the disk and liner page, they do store a lot! Some hold over 400! If you absolutely want the original hard plastic jacket with it, there are other storage concepts. The welded wire organizers are inexpensive and durable. Some are oriented horizontally, and some vertically. I see these things at consumer electronics stores and discount retailers. There are also a variety of shelf units that hold CDs and DVDs in the original jackets. Most have some kind of sliding stop to hold them upright. These cost a little more. Some look quite attractive, but not all. They are the bulkiest option.

Vacuum bags come in a few different sizes. They work by vacuuming out the air. This can really compress bulky sweaters and down comforters.

Multiplex hangers hold several garments in less than normal space. The welded steel units are obviously more durable and costly than the plastic ones. I get a lot of mileage out of the pants hanger and the belt hanger.

I would like to recommend that you get a small lock box, or safe, for valuables. No one carries all these with them all the time. Whether it is a debit card, cash, bonds, jewelry, thesis manuscript, etc., keep it safe! If it is important to you, lock it up! Better safe than sorry.

The following storage concepts will work as a stand alone item. At first glance they would seem more suited to an apartment or a house than a dormitory, but one of these might help you.

Closet enhancement systems can be purchased as components or as kits. They are an assortment of closet rods and shelves at different heights, plus hooks, bins and drawers. These can maximize the storage potential of a small closet.

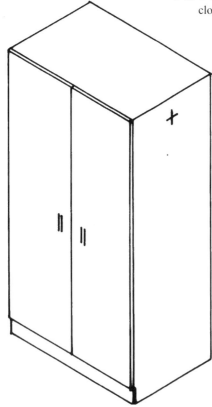

A wardrobe is a large portable cabinet for storing clothes. Wardrobes can be plain or decorative; made from wood, particle board, molded plastic or sheet metal. These are usually 3' or 4' wide, and 6' tall, (90 cm–20 cm x 2 m). Wardrobes are essentially a small closet. They are usually inexpensive. They completely hide the contents when closed. They are typically shipped unassembled.

Garment racks come in many sizes, shapes and configurations. Most are made from light metal tubing, although wood, plastic and wire shelves may be incorporated in the design. Most can be moved on castors. Garment racks are usually inexpensive. They don't conceal the contents, nor keep dust off of them.

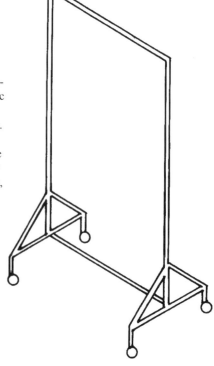

Over Door Robe Hook

Door hangers are storage devices that hang from the top edge of a door. These may be robe hooks, towel bars or specialty shelving for shoes or products. They are inexpensive and fairly durable. The hanger portion is a hook made from thin flat metal strapping. No holes, nails or screws are required to mount them. There are similar storage devices available with out the hooks, which do require fasteners. Most dormitories and landlords don't allow holes in their doors.

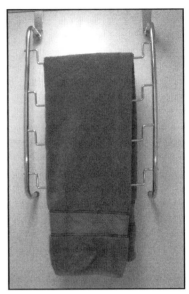
Over Door Towel Bar

Utility shelving could be metal or plastic. There is quite a price, appearance, and quality range. Some look industrial, some reference commercial kitchens, and others perhaps a toy room. These can hold a lot of stackable contents, or containers of loose items. Again, everything is visible.

Portable kitchen storage may be free standing cabinetry, carts, or racks. Basically, these have a small counter top, some storage space, and possibly some display area. A towel drying bar is a nice addition. The illustration sequence shows the progression from small cabinets to large, and from a single feature to several. The largest item; a "baker rack", has all of the desired features. It can greatly enhance a kitchenette. These are typically about 3' wide, 18" deep, and 5' high, (1 m x 50 cm x 150 m).

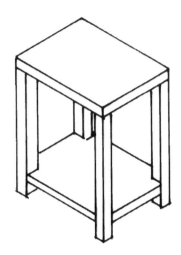 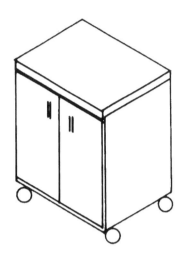 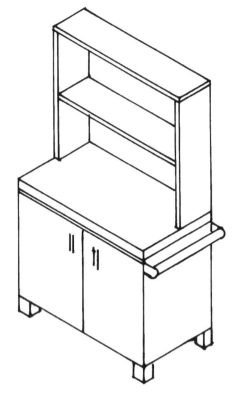

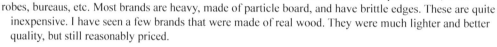

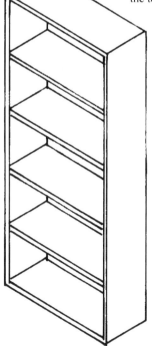

Knock down premanufactured furniture requires some assembly. It is held together with knockdown hardware, hence the term. A really wide variety of furniture types are available in this; bookshelves, computer desks, wardrobes, bureaus, etc. Most brands are heavy, made of particle board, and have brittle edges. These are quite inexpensive. I have seen a few brands that were made of real wood. They were much lighter and better quality, but still reasonably priced.

Unpainted furniture works for a lot of people. The entire gamut of furniture types is available. Most are pretty decent quality. Of course you have to finish it yourself! Paint it, or stain-varnish? By now you should be highly skilled at varnishing…

Used furniture stores, auctions, private sales, etc., can offer great deals. You should already know what the fair value is when negotiating the price. Your bargaining confidence is much stronger if you know what the top price should be. There are also a few unscrupulous sellers who would cheat you if they can. Fore warned is fore armed.

Accepting used upholstered furniture is risky. Obviously mattresses can be unsanitary, but couches and recliners too! Any of these can be infested with bugs or mice. Even as a gift, it is a risk. Be suspicious of holes and stains. If the bottom liner is torn or missing, don't take it! You don't have to learn everything the hard way. Some things are as easy as following the voice of experience. Sure, mice or insects may come with the apartment or dorm, but you don't need to invite them in! Learning exterminator skills is not necessarily required in the curriculum. Avoiding and preventing may be just as good.

I hope you have got enough ideas now to make the most of your new living space. Good luck to you.

STANDARDS AND REGULATIONS

Consumer Products Safety Commission: cpsc.org

American Society of Testing and Materials: astm.org

Applicable standards for temporary wiring, cables and cords:
NEC, NEMA, IEC, and UL

Fire safety standards for paint, furnishings and mattresses:
NFPA.org, BHFTI.org, and ULstandards.org

APPENDIX B

SPECIALTY VENDORS

Benjaminmoore.com sells a fire retardant paint

A few laminated foam mattress suppliers:
IKEA.com, target.com, and sleepmemoryfoam.com

A few sources of shelving and containers:
Metro.com, elfa.com , IKEA.com

Many over the door hardware items can be found at:
acehardware.com , elfa.com, and homedepot.com